The Good News for the Liturgical Community
Cycle A

Valentino Del Mazza, S.D.B.

St. Paul Editions

IMPRIMI POTEST:
   Rev. D. Eugenio Valentini, S.D.B.

NIHIL OBSTAT:
   Rev. Richard V. Lawlor, S.J.
   Censor Deputatus

IMPRIMATUR:
   +Humberto Cardinal Medeiros
   Archbishop of Boston

Translated by Robert John Bosse

Solemnities and feast days are in volume C of this series.

Observations regarding the quotations used in the text:

The Bible text in this publication is from the *Revised Standard Version Bible* (modified form), *Catholic Edition*, copyrighted © 1965 and 1966 by the Division of Christian Education of the National Council of the Churches of Christ in the U.S.A., and is used by permission.

Excerpts from addresses of Pope Paul VI and Pope John Paul II have been taken with permission from the texts as published in the weekly English editions of *L'Osservatore Romano*, the official publication of Vatican City.

Excerpts from the documents of Vatican Council II have been taken from the N.C. translations appearing in *The Sixteen Documents of Vatican II*, St. Paul Editions.

Library of Congress Cataloging in Publication Data

Del Mazza, Valentino.
   The good news for the liturgical community.
   Translation of La buona novella per l'assemblea liturgica.
   CONTENTS: [1] Cycle A.—[2] Cycle B.—[3] Cycle C and liturgical feasts of cycles A, B, C.
   1. Church year—Meditations.   I. Title.
BX2170.C55D4413   242'.3   80-10138

ISBN 0-8198-3011-9 (v. 1)
ISBN 0-8198-3012-7 (pbk. : v. 1)

Copyright © 1981, by the Daughters of St. Paul

Printed in the U.S.A. by the Daughters of St. Paul
50 St. Paul's Ave., Boston, MA 02130

The Daughters of St. Paul are an international congregation of religious women serving the Church with the communications media.

To my Catholic friends in America

CONTENTS

Valentino del Mazza: A Biographical Note 11
Preface 13
First Sunday of Advent:
    COME, LORD, AND FREE US 15
Second Sunday of Advent:
    THE SEVEN GIFTS OF THE HOLY SPIRIT 17
Third Sunday of Advent:
    RECLAIMING HOPE 21
Fourth Sunday of Advent:
    MARY IN THE HISTORY OF SALVATION 24
Christmas:
    CHRISTMAS 29
Holy Family:
    ELDERLY PEOPLE 32
January 1, Solemnity of the Mother of God:
    MARY: AN EXAMPLE FOR MEDITATION 36
Second Sunday after Christmas:
    CREATION AND ELEVATION TO THE
        SUPERNATURAL 40
The Epiphany of the Lord:
    A FESTIVITY OF LIGHT 42
Baptism of the Lord:
    BAPTISM 45
First Sunday of Lent:
    THE ORIGIN OF MANKIND AND SIN 48
Second Sunday of Lent:
    FAITH: RISKS AND PROMISES 51
Third Sunday of Lent:
    GRACE 55
Fourth Sunday of Lent:
    THE PEDAGOGY OF FAITH 58
Fifth Sunday of Lent:
    THE RESURRECTION OF THE BODY 61

Passion Sunday (Palm Sunday):
    THE PASSION OF OUR LORD 64
Easter Sunday:
    THE RESURRECTION OF OUR LORD 67
Second Sunday of Easter:
    THE SACRAMENT OF PENANCE 70
Third Sunday of Easter:
    WE ARE PILGRIMS 73
Fourth Sunday of Easter:
    AUTHORITY IN THE CHURCH 77
Fifth Sunday of Easter:
    THE PRIESTHOOD OF THE FAITHFUL 80
Sixth Sunday of Easter:
    THE SACRAMENT OF CONFIRMATION 82
Ascension Thursday:
    THE ASCENSION OF THE LORD................ 85
Seventh Sunday of Easter:
    PRAYER AND THE CHURCH.................... 88
Pentecost Sunday:
    THE HOLY SPIRIT AND RENEWAL 91
Trinity Sunday:
    THE TRINITY IN OUR HISTORY AND OUR LIVES .. 94
The Feast of *Corpus Christi:*
    THE BREAD OF ANGELS 97
Second Sunday in Ordinary Time:
    SANCTITY IS THE GOAL OF RELIGION 100
Third Sunday in Ordinary Time:
    DEMONSTRATION AND COMMUNION IN
        THE CHURCH 102
Fourth Sunday in Ordinary Time:
    THE DYNAMICS OF THE BEATITUDES 104
Fifth Sunday in Ordinary Time:
    THE APOSTOLIC COMMITMENT
        OF THE PEOPLE OF GOD 108
Sixth Sunday in Ordinary Time:
    CHRIST, THE LAW, AND LOVE 111
Seventh Sunday in Ordinary Time:
    LOVE AND ENEMIES 113
Eighth Sunday in Ordinary Time:
    DIVINE FIDELITY AND HUMAN TRUST 116
Ninth Sunday in Ordinary Time:
    THE ESSENCE OF CHRISTIAN LIFE 118
Tenth Sunday in Ordinary Time:
    THE MERCY OF GOD 121
Eleventh Sunday in Ordinary Time:
    THE BLOOD OF CHRIST 123

Twelfth Sunday in Ordinary Time:
    THE APOSTOLATE AND PERSECUTION 125
Thirteenth Sunday in Ordinary Time:
    HOSPITALITY 128
Fourteenth Sunday in Ordinary Time:
    THE THEOLOGY OF HUMILITY 131
Fifteenth Sunday in Ordinary Time:
    EVANGELIZATION AND THE WORD OF GOD 133
Sixteenth Sunday in Ordinary Time:
    CATECHISM FOR CHILDREN 136
Seventeenth Sunday in Ordinary Time:
    THE COVENANT AND GOD'S LOVE 138
Eighteenth Sunday in Ordinary Time:
    HUNGER IN THE WORLD 140
Nineteenth Sunday in Ordinary Time:
    THE THEOLOGY OF CRISIS IN THE CHURCH 144
Twentieth Sunday in Ordinary Time:
    THE UNIVERSALITY OF THE CHURCH 148
Twenty-first Sunday in Ordinary Time:
    THE CHURCH AND PETER 151
Twenty-second Sunday in Ordinary Time:
    THE WAY OF THE CROSS 154
Twenty-third Sunday in Ordinary Time:
    DIALOGUE AND FRATERNAL CORRECTION 157
Twenty-fourth Sunday in Ordinary Time:
    VIOLENCE AND PARDON 159
Twenty-fifth Sunday in Ordinary Time:
    THE CALL OF GOD AND LOVE 162
Twenty-sixth Sunday in Ordinary Time:
    VIRTUE AND CIVILIZATION 164
Twenty-seventh Sunday in Ordinary Time:
    CHRISTIAN HUMANISM 167
Twenty-eighth Sunday in Ordinary Time:
    THE CATHOLIC CHURCH AND OTHER RELIGIONS 169
Twenty-ninth Sunday in Ordinary Time:
    RELIGION AND POLITICS 173
Thirtieth Sunday in Ordinary Time:
    THE DYNAMICS AND PERFECTION OF ALTRUISM 175
Thirty-first Sunday in Ordinary Time:
    THE PROBLEMS OF THE PRIESTHOOD 177
Thirty-second Sunday in Ordinary Time:
    DEATH AND THE CHRISTIAN 180
Thirty-third Sunday in Ordinary Time:
    THE SPIRITUAL QUALITIES OF WOMEN 182
Christ the King:
    CHRIST HAS RISEN FOR ALL TIMES 186

VALENTINO DEL MAZZA:
A Biographical Note

Professor Valentino Del Mazza, S.D.B., a Tuscan, is presently residing in Rome at the Salesian Pontifical University.

He is a doctor in Sacred Theology and is the author of the following books: *La Famiglia nel Pensiero di Pio XII* (The Family According to the Mind of Pius XII); *Forza del Sesso Debole* (Strength of the Weaker Sex); *Maternità* (Motherhood); *Amarsi* (Mutual Love); *Cielo Sereno* (Clear Skies); *L'Ideale del Cristiano* (The Christian Ideal); *Il Canto dell'Anima* (The Song of the Soul); *La Pasqua della Morte Cristiana* (The Easter of Christian Death); and *La Madonna* (Our Lady Among Us). He has also compiled the three volumes of sermons for the Liturgical Year A, B, C. He has also produced a number of shorter works. Not a few of the above-mentioned titles have been translated into foreign languages, namely Spanish, Portuguese and Japanese.

He is a member of various Academies and is a gazetted journalist. He is, for many years, a correspondent of Vatican Radio. He is, above all, the Director of the Moral and Religious Advisory Board at the Salesian University, and throughout Italy he is a well-known preacher and lecturer.

"The literary style of Father Del Mazza unfolds gradually and as it takes shape it releases a broad outlook. It is fluent and at the same time incisive.... His historical and biblical references are immediately followed by convincing arguments which appear to be a mere whisper on the lips of a true friend. It is precisely this unique, intelligent, free yet profound style of his that reaches us. He masters that simplicity which teaches us the value of joy—a joy we so heedlessly allow to escape from our grasp" (Florence Radio, January 25, 1961 and June 14, 1962). "It is that unique Tuscan style which bears a touch of freshness, with a delightful, rich ,and varied vocabulary. His thoughts unravel, as it were, in spiral fashion, in concentric circles, inviting us to pursue its novelty and depth. It is also unique in its prompt ethical and spiritual expression" (Vatican Radio, November 10, 1973). "...a brilliant and enticing style...which can be compared with real poetry and fascinating imagery" (Vatican Radio, May 1, 1975).

PREFACE

It is indeed a pleasure to present the latest of Reverend Valentino Del Mazza. In true Salesian spirit, like St. John Bosco, Father Valentino is relentless in his efforts to diffuse good literature.

This volume "A Cycle" is the first of a series covering the three years. *The Good News for the Liturgical Community* is the clear and organized collection of thoughts and reflections which Father Valentino presented on the Vatican Radio where his precious collaboration is valued and appreciated.

The fundamental merit of this book is its doctrinal value. The author, like every authentic theologian, always begins with the Scriptures and the teaching authority of the Church. Father Valentino so enriches his book with an abundance of well-chosen words of the late Vicar of Christ, Pope Paul VI, that we could retitle this volume "The Liturgy of the Word according to the teachings of Pope Paul VI."

Reverend Valentino has a pleasant adeptness to integrate his philosophical, psychological, historical, catechetical, and pastoral knowledge with Revelation. The topics are frequently theoretical and difficult; nevertheless, each meditation is a lively conversation which anyone can follow.

This volume will certainly be appreciated by priests who desire new material for Sunday homilies, catechism classes, and conferences; it will be an abundant source of reflection for all those consecrated souls who make meditation a part of their way of life; and it will be a valid assistance to all who wish to enjoy the truth and the light of Christ.

John Giorgionni, S.J.
Director of the VATICAN RADIO: Italian Section
Rome: July 31, 1977

FIRST SUNDAY OF ADVENT

Come, Lord, and Free Us

Readings: Isaiah 2:1-5
Romans 13:11-14
Matthew 24:37-44

The history of man is a story of the search for God. Man can be constantly surrounded by people and yet he is lonesome. This loneliness drives man to seek the supernatural. "Man is never completely satisfied because he feels the need to go elsewhere, towards Someone" (Luis Veuillot). Every human being experiences this vertical tension, for it cannot be denied; it is in man's nature.

The goal of man's life is to find God; that He exists is not doubted: "thirst is a clear demonstration that water exists." To meet God is possible and easy. God seeks man to make him completely free.

Both in the Old and the New Testaments each time God reveals Himself to man He does so with a plan of freedom. His very name indicates a "God who saves: who frees" (cf. Exodus 3:6; 6:2; Isaiah 43:10; 48:12). It is not a strange coincidence that God's chosen people live in constant hope of being freed from every type of slavery, for the original hope of the chosen people was to be freed from slavery in Egypt.

With time and experience, freedom—as other truths —has passed from a predominantly social and occasional event to a constant moral state. In the New Testament, the word "liberation" takes on a precise and complete meaning in the person of Christ. Who is Christ? Christian faith presents Him as the Son of God made man; the Messiah we have waited for; the Savior of the world; our Teacher; the joy of the world; the image of the invisible God; the Truth, the Life and the Way (cf. John 14:6); our friend (cf. John 15:14-15). Christ knows our thoughts (cf. Luke 6:8); He can console us (cf. John 20:13), forgive us (cf. Matthew 9:12), heal us (cf. Luke 6:19), and raise us from the dead (cf. Luke 7:14; John 11:43). He will return to judge all mankind (cf. Matthew 25:31). Christ frees us from all sin. He is the object of our desires, our daily bread. No man can live without Him. Everyone can be His friend. He is the light of mankind.

Saints Paul and John give us the theory of our spiritual liberation. St. Paul insists that our liberation has taken place through Christ (cf. Galatians 5:1-13; 4:26-31) and through His love for us (cf. Romans 7:24). St. John gives us the means with which to achieve this freedom and truth (cf. John 8:32-36).

PASTORAL REFLECTIONS

1. *The presence of God and friendship with Him is the goal of every human being.* At birth we were cared for by a loving mother and provided for by an affectionate father. We were bathed in love and care; we did not know those near us, yet we were aware of their loving, freeing presence. As we grew up, we came to know the beauty of life, the wonders of creation, the marvels of goodness and joy. It is not possible to know everything, but it is easy to see the presence and love of God in our lives. It is not a question of giving God a certain control

over our lives; we need God. God calls us to rise above our nature, to free ourselves from finite and contingent structures, to be His friends, and at the same time He comes to us to give us His life.

2. *God does not impose this message of freedom; He respects our freedom.* Niceta Stetato, a humble monk of the eleventh century, wrote: "When God created man He gave him a free will, and after enriching man with intelligence he placed life and death before him" (cf. Deuteronomy 30:19). The Lord said: "He who is not with me is against me, and he who does not gather with me scatters" (Luke 11:23). We are to adhere to Christ with our entire personality.

3. *There is a moral alternative in our lives,* the choice between good and evil. The Bible figuratively speaks of this alternative as the "two ways." There is the way of virtue and sanctity and the way of vice and evil (cf. Micah 6:8; John 14:6). To walk the path of virtue means to live Christ. The idea is not new, for Isaiah long ago extended an invitation: "Come, let us climb the Lord's mountain, to the house of the God of Jacob, that he may instruct us in his ways and we may walk in his paths" (First Reading). Let us pray frequently with the psalmist, "Show us, O Lord, your mercy and give us your salvation" (Responsorial Psalm).

SECOND SUNDAY OF ADVENT

The Seven Gifts of the Holy Spirit

Readings: Isaiah 11:1-10
Romans 15:4-9
Matthew 3:1-12

The freedom which comes from God is an internal freedom; it works under the influence of the Holy Spirit. Any positive transformation of man comes through the work of the Holy Spirit. This is the constant teaching of the Scriptures, of Tradition, of the Liturgy, and of Vatican Council II. The Holy Spirit invades and transforms man's spirit with His seven gifts: "The Spirit of the Lord shall rest upon him, the spirit of wisdom and understanding, the spirit of counsel and might, the spirit of knowledge and the fear of the Lord" (Isaiah 11:2).

The Fathers and Doctors of the Church and, in particular, Saints Augustine and Thomas took delight in relating the effects of the Holy Spirit to the number seven: e.g., the seven requests in the "Our Father." Isaiah uses various expressions to stress the fact that the Holy Spirit effectively invades our entire nature. It is evident, however, that it is only one gift. A ray of light is broken into seven colors, harmony into seven notes. The infinite Lord of the Holy Spirit remains undivided, yet acquires dynamic modulations conforming to the faculties of the receiver. This single gift becomes wisdom, when it enables us to distinguish between eternal and temporal reality; understanding when it enables us to distinguish between what is true and false; counsel when it helps us to decide what is the correct thing to do and what is good to omit. Fortitude helps the Christian overcome the difficulties of his everyday life. Knowledge, which is similar to understanding, renders us docile to God's teaching. Piety makes us available for the joyful service of praising God, and fear urges respect for God, our infinitely just Father.

The Holy Spirit is a loving revolution in our personality. Who gives us the strength to remain silent when we have been hurt or offended? Who urges us to forgive even when our pardon can be misinterpreted? Who gives us the strength to obey when we know that acting otherwise would be more profitable? Why is it that we do not feel completely alone when abandoned by friends or at the loss of loved ones? How can we explain that secret conviction that truth will prevail in spite of the disbelief of others? Where do we obtain courage to make great sacrifices knowing that they will always remain a secret? Who gives us an insight to eternal values while most prefer temporal values? As the years pass, how do we explain our interior enthusiasm and supernatural optimism? Without the Holy Spirit there is no answer to any of these questions.

Reinhard Johannes Sorge once said: "All that is good in us comes from the Holy Spirit, while that which is bad is our own. Evil desires, faults and shortcomings are mine; while grace, the desire of good, the gift of loyalty and the glory of a pure heart are all gifts of your Spirit!" St. Augustine wrote: "The grace of the Holy Spirit enables us to know what is good and do it; it is through the Holy Spirit that we can believe and love and thus obtain the strength to act in accordance with what we believe."

On the supernatural level the gifts of the Holy Spirit are magnificent and complete. We are born sons of God through the Holy Spirit. Almost by instinct we feel that Christ is truly the Son of God, but in reality it is by a gift of the Holy Spirit. If we must witness the Lord with our lives, it is the Holy Spirit who gives us the strength. Invisibly and mysteriously the Spirit transforms our likeness to God into an image of Christ, so that we can fully live His life and glory (cf. Galatians 2:20; Romans 8:2-10). It is only through the Holy Spirit that we can perceive that God dwells in us with His grace, and it is the same Spirit who intercedes for us, giving voice to our requests as adopted sons of God. Those who receive the Holy Spirit become part of the Church; St. Irenaeus of Lyons, in fact, wrote: "Where the Church is, there also is the Holy Spirit, and where the Holy Spirit is, there is the Church and grace."

PASTORAL REFLECTIONS

1. It should be quite clear that the multiple manifestations of Christian life are necessarily connected to the capacity that we have of receiving the Holy Spirit. *In fact, a Christian is one who is totally available to the Holy Spirit.* All things follow laws: the minerals obey the

laws of gravitation; the plants, the laws of chemistry; the animals follow their instincts; man follows his intellect and will, but the Christian is guided by the Holy Spirit (cf. Romans 8:14).

2. *An apostle is simply one sent by the Holy Spirit.* With the strength of the Holy Spirit one can overcome all doubts about what he has to do, the decisions he has to make, the sufferings he must undergo for the glory of God and the salvation of others. St. Matthew gives us an excellent example: St. John the Baptist (cf. Third Reading). We also have the example of the Apostles. They had lived in constant contact with Christ. They saw His miracles; they were inspired by His conversations; they were enthusiastic about Christ. Nevertheless they were afraid and abandoned Him during His passion. Even after His resurrection Christ had to reproach them for their doubts. All this was before Pentecost. With the descent of the Holy Spirit they were transformed. They witnessed to Christ at the cost of their lives. St. Gregory the Great said: "The Holy Spirit descended on Christ in the form of a dove to indicate his kindness to sinners; He descended on the Apostles in the form of tongues of fire, so that they could fill the world with the fire of God's love."

3. *Saints are those who live the action of the Holy Spirit.* St. Thérèse of the Child Jesus had a picture of Christ with the Samaritan woman at the well. She would frequently pray before this picture that the Holy Spirit would descend upon her. It was this divine Spirit who planted and nourished the desire for simplicity and heavenly values in this small girl. The Curé of Ars found it very difficult to complete his studies for the priesthood. He nevertheless became the counselor of priests, bishops and lords. All of France wanted him as their confessor. There can be only one explanation for this: the work of the Holy Spirit. St. Thomas Aquinas had no problem in explaining the action of the Holy Spirit as an insight which is superior to reason. The Christian personality is saturated by the action of the Third Person of the Trinity.

THIRD SUNDAY OF ADVENT

Reclaiming Hope

Readings: Isaiah 35:1-6, 10
Jeremiah 5:7-10
Matthew 11:2-11

There is an important problem to solve: regain hope (cf. First and Second Readings).

Christian hope is not the fruit of a psychological desire to meet the anxieties of everyday life, nor is it an idealistic projection of the future to reduce the harshness of reality. Theological hope is not something occasional, nor does it depend on our emotional state. Rather, it is a permanent and essential dimension of our religious attitude. Christian hope is a sublime gift of God. We do not create it; we receive it, and it qualifies us as members of God's family.

Hope is a supernatural richness and, consequently, rational evaluations fail to fathom it; it is beyond intellectual research. Once hope is realized, it is no longer hope: it is possession. In fact, theological hope seems to be a paradox: to trust even when human hope has disappeared (cf. Romans 4:18). In this case hope is equivalent to abandoning human abilities, to a refusal to trust in oneself. In other words, it is an attitude of radical humility which prepares us for God's gratuitous intervention.

Let us consider the meaning of the word "hope": to trust in God, to long for, to rely on, to desire, to love. It is easy to see how hope is related to faith and charity. St. Paul clearly relates these three virtues: faith, hope and charity (cf. 1 Thessalonians 1:13; 1 Corinthians 13:13; Galatians 5:5).

The history of faith united to hope begins with Abraham in the Old Testament. Abraham faces the future because he trusts that God will keep His promises; he hopes because he firmly believes in the word of God. God demands the sacrifice of Isaac, and in that very moment Abraham's faith is complete and his hope is perfect. Abraham is the spiritual type of the future people of God.

In the New Testament we have the Virgin Mary who fully accepts the divine message, certain that God will fulfill His promise in spite of the contrary historic indications. In the early Church the Apostles believe because they hope, and they trust because they believe what was revealed to them.

Through the Incarnation and the descent of the Holy Spirit, hope becomes overflowing charity which is identified with love. Even if the Church is still involved in the drama of historic reality, this divine love is substantially diffused throughout the Church. The desire is that it be complete and definite. This desire is simply expressed in the Aramaic prayer of early Christianity: *"Maranatha:* Come, Lord Jesus" (cf. 1 Corinthians 16:22; Revelation 22:20).

At this point someone could object that a Christian is one who gives up everything. It is interesting to explore the bonds between hope and love in their horizontal dimension, that is, in relation to others. Nowhere does the Bible mention egoistic hope. It considers only the hope which is beneficial to others. What is hoped for is hoped also for our brethren (cf. 2 Corinthians 1:7). Hope arouses a control of and separation from earthly reality. At the same time hope urges us to use and share this reality for the happiness of others in view of the future good (cf. 1 Thessalonians 5:8; 1 Peter 1:13; 4:17). The essential paradox of hope is this: it is both total insecurity and undoubted trust, it is unshakable certainty of victory and fearful vigilance so as not to betray our vocation to be authors of history. It is a promise and at the same time a reality; it is completely illuminated by the future and constantly informed by experiences of the past. It is a totally personal gift and gratuitous action for community life. It is an entirely divine quality in its origin and human in its marvelous social effects. Hope for the Christian does not mean to flee from the world but to give the life of Christ's kingdom to earthly reality. Christian hope is a constant love which penetrates everything, relating everything to man, master of the cosmos, directing everything to Christ, the final goal of our lives. Origen said: "The Christian is a full citizen of earth and at the same time a temporary guest in this world." St. Augustine put it in another way: "To be yourself, transcend time!"

PASTORAL REFLECTIONS

1. *Hope generates absolute historic certainty in God's promises:* Catholic theology demonstrates how the Old Testament was fully realized in the Person of Christ. The prophecies related to the time and place of His birth, to His mother, to His forerunner John the Baptist, were all completely fulfilled. Christ's prophecies, such as His betrayal by Judas, Peter's denial, His passion and resurrection, the destruction of Jerusalem, the conversion of pagans and the propagation and duration of the Church, were all fulfilled with surprising precision. There is no reason to doubt that what the Lord has promised will come to be.

2. *Trust goes hand in hand with optimism.* Hope enables us to see our history in a new light—optimistically—even if suffering remains. In chapter 35 of his prophecies Isaiah gives us an excellent example:

"The wilderness and the dry land shall be glad,
   the desert shall rejoice and blossom....
Then the eyes of the blind shall be opened,
   and the ears of the deaf unstopped;
then shall the lame man leap like a hart,
   and the tongue of the dumb sing for joy.
And a highway shall be there,
   and it shall be called the Holy Way;
   ...the redeemed shall walk there.
And the ransomed of the Lord shall return,
   and come to Zion with singing;

everlasting joy shall be upon their heads;
 they shall obtain joy and gladness,
 and sorrow and sighing shall flee away."

(Isaiah 35:1, 5-6, 8-10)

In the dimension of hope we can achieve maturity. The coercive motivation to bring about a better life is found in hope, both on a personal and historic level. The Christian who is nourished by hope and lives constantly and generously in the present will be able to overcome his egoism, to transform his work and to restore human and cosmic reality (cf. Past. Const.: Church in the Modern World, no. 48).

FOURTH SUNDAY OF ADVENT

Mary in the History of Salvation

Readings: Isaiah 7:10-14
Romans 1:1-7
Matthew 1:18-24

The Madonna's role in our salvation is present throughout the liturgical year. During Advent and in particular on the Fourth Sunday this role is more explicit.

The important position of the Virgin in the plan of redemption is contained in the promise of salvation (cf. Genesis 3:15). The New Testament pursues this concept. St. Mark begins with memories of Mary. St. Matthew centralizes her importance as the one who will become the Mother of God through the action of the Holy Spirit (cf. Third Reading). St. Luke places her first, and St. John has Christ begin and end His public life with Mary: the wedding feast at Cana and the scene on Calvary, thus indicating Mary's mission and importance. It is also St. John who has the Woman battle with the Evil

One during the last stage of the Church (cf. Revelation 12). Scripture begins and ends with Mary.

These limited data in the New Testament were the fertile seed which developed into the present Marian doctrine and devotion. Tradition, liturgy, history, hagiography, the Church's teaching—both conciliar and pontifical—are constantly more and more Marian. Vatican II, in its Constitution on the Sacred Liturgy, states: "In celebrating this annual cycle of Christ's mysteries, holy Church honors with special love the Blessed Mary, Mother of God, who is joined by an inseparable bond to the saving work of her Son. In her the Church holds up and admires the most excellent fruit of Redemption and joyfully contemplates, as a faultless model, that which she herself desires and hopes to be" (Const. on the Sacred Liturgy, no. 103). She is the beginning, the image and the mother of the Church until the pilgrimage to the future era is completed (cf. Dogmatic Constitution on the Church, no. 68).

Pope Paul issued an important document on Marian cult (Feb. 2, 1974). In its 58 articles the Pope propounds, orients and proclaims the devotion to the Madonna.

There are many valid objective motives which justify the central reference to Mary. We will recall some of those which unite the Virgin to God's marvelous plan of salvation. The Madonna was created "perfectly beautiful in her soul" so that she could cooperate with God; she is Immaculate. St. Lawrence of Brindisi wrote: "From the first man, Adam, God formed the first woman. From the second Woman, God produced the second Man, Christ; the first from the earth, the second from heaven. They say that the sun is formed from the purest part of the heavens: Christ, the sun of justice, is formed from the purest of earthly creatures." The Immaculate Virgin is God's masterpiece.

Pope Paul VI said: "Mary is the annunciation of salvation. Mary is the immediate preparation which crowns and completes the development of the divine plan of redemption. She is the fulfillment of the prophecies; she is the key to understand the mysterious Messianic messages; she is the point of arrival of God's thought" (Paul VI, Sept. 8, 1965).

It is important to remember that God created Mary Immaculate because in her and from her, life would flow in its integrity and purity, and also because she would be our Mediatrix. Her redemptive mediation is not parallel and integral to that of her Son as if Christ produced 99% and the Madonna 1%. Her mediation is cooperative and subordinated. It is not a side-by-side cooperation, but one within the other. A comparison might be useful. A pen contributes its 100% in writing even if the person writing, qualitatively different from the pen, also contributes 100%. The Madonna, like the subordinate instrument, cooperates in all her dimensions. St. Andrew of Crete greets her as "the dispenser of grace and the life of the living" and St. John Damascene as "the cause and dispenser of every good." This concept is later diffused during the Middle Ages by St. Bernard of Clairvaux.

Mary is the "Mother of the Church." This is the more dynamic characteristic of the Virgin and the reason for the sincere and affectionate veneration of the Christian people. Even if this truth has been proclaimed only recently (Pope Paul VI—Nov. 21, 1964), it is as old as the Church. The Madonna becomes effectively the Mother of the Church in the very moment of the Incarnation; she reveals herself as such on Calvary. She begins her ecclesial maternity on Pentecost and continues to be the Mother of the entire Mystical Body of Christ. Christian writers, saints and preachers have spoken of Mary, Mother of the Church, in many ways. St. Hilary of Arles wrote: "The Church is the creature of God, and Mary is its beginning." Cromazio, Bishop of Aquileia and a good friend of St. Jerome, once said: "Let us go to the home of Mary, to the Church of Christ, where Mary the Mother of the Lord lives. In fact, the Church lives with Mary. It is not possible to speak of the Church if the Mother of Jesus is not present with His brothers, that is, with the Apostles..." (cf. Sermons 29, 20). Esichius, a priest and monk in Jerusalem, wrote: "The Church has the Virgin Mother of God as its heart. In fact, as the principal part of every living thing is the soul, in like manner, Christ dwells in the Madonna, Mother of God, as in a heart, that Christ who is the life of the faithful." One of the most expressive comments on the relation between Mary and the Church is that of Blessed Isaac, Abbot of the Monastery of Stella (France). He wrote: "Mary and the Church are both Virgins and Mothers. They both conceive without sin through the work of the Holy Spirit; the Virgin conceives the Head, the Church continues to conceive the members. Both are Mothers, and neither can give birth without the other. This is why the Scriptures and the Liturgy attribute these concepts to the Virgin and the Church. What is universally attributed to the Church and specifically to the Virgin can be individually attributed to our souls, sanctified by the Spirit and capable of generating Christ. Christ lived in the Virgin for nine months, in order to live until the consummation of time in the Church and to live eternally in knowledge and love in each soul."

PASTORAL REFLECTIONS

1. *Mary will lead us to God.* The Madonna is inseparably united to God (cf. Third Reading). God wants to meet man and Mary prepares the way, just as Moses led the chosen people towards the promised land (cf. Micah 6:4). Mary is the salvific epiphany of God. God wanted to dwell in Mary not only once but always, so that man could find God in a completely human way. Mary is the door through which God comes to us and we go to God. Every encounter with Mary is an encounter with Jesus. Father Faber, a convert from Anglicanism, once said: "I was able to find and love Jesus only after I placed my heart in the heart of Mary."

2. In our Catholic mentality, proper importance should be given to the conviction that the Madonna urges us to *make ourselves at home in the Church.*

Christ has three generations: within the Father, within the Virgin and within the Church. From the Father He is born always, from the Virgin He was born once, in the Church He is frequently born. The first is a divine generation, the second is human and the third is mystical or the generation of sanctity, all three are inseparably united. Mary is the connection between the first and the third generations. Without her we are practically orphans, that is, we would be without certain supernatural Christian values.

DECEMBER 25
CHRISTMAS (MASS DURING THE DAY)

Christmas

Readings: Isaiah 52:7-10
Hebrews 1:1-6
John 1:1-18

Christmas is full of marvels. The greatest joy comes from the fact that the Savior is born. God is now with us, like us and here to help us. "This day in David's city a Savior has been born to you, the Messiah and Lord" (Luke 2:12). The story of man is the story of a dream, a desire, a need to communicate with God: man's vocation is to love God. Man's efforts had been in vain partly because of his weakness as a creature and partly because the finite could never possess the infinite without the mysterious initiative of the infinite. Finally, man's desire is fulfilled, God comes to live with us. We all can now reach God, because God is with us. We all can now reach God, because God is made Man. "Remember how man was far from God, but through Christ we can now reach God, be His friends, and fully satisfy our desire" (St. Augustine).

The beginning of the reign of divine love seems to be a paradox: sinners can become friends of God. We will be able to comprehend this only when we see God face to face. If God would evaluate love in our terms, He would never come to us, for we simply do not merit it; nor could we withstand His infinite perfection. Instead He is born an infant because we are small and weak. We are easily attracted to this Child. Only divine wisdom could find this marvelous way to reconcile man. The Infant born in Bethlehem is so small and yet the Omnipresent, so weak and yet the Omnipotent, so poor and yet the King of the universe. But more than anything that Child is so lovable!

The birth of Christ is the beginning of the history of "man's new heart." Jesus brought love to each individual, to the family and to society. Christmas transforms our homes, fills them with joy. Communication with those near us becomes easier and more sincere; loneliness and suffering are less intense. Whatever we do today to lessen the anxiety, loneliness or suffering of others is simply an anticipation of the goodness of God made Man. The love which flows from Bethlehem transforms the hearts of those who suffer, because God now lives and suffers with us and for us.

Children are of particular importance in the celebration of Christmas; they are the center of the family as the Child Jesus is. As long as there are children, we know that God loves the world and that our history will continue. God is born an infant because He wants to renew and bless life at its very source.

Christmas invites us to verify who we are. We all feel the need to remain young at heart. To be ourselves we desire to live the extraordinary moments of our lives in an ordinary way. We long for the simplicity of Bethlehem. We feel the need to smile more frequently, to be free, to express wonder and awe, to be able to get excited over little things which reveal the presence of God.

It is essential for us to regain our natural candor, that ability to enjoy the simple things of life, to see beauty in everything. The magnificent scene of Bethlehem is a confirmation that our Christian life is a marvelous gift.

PASTORAL REFLECTIONS

1. *We should go to Bethlehem with the shepherds.* Our vital relationship with Christ is renewed at Christmas. The Child Jesus is born to draw all men to Himself. A newborn child has an irresistible attraction. Christ calls us and invites us to be His friends. Who has accepted this invitation to "go over to Bethlehem with the shepherds?" Those who enjoy Christmas as an encounter with the Word of God made Man; those who suffer and are afflicted and find consolation in Him alone; those innocent and ordinary people who feel the presence of God even if they cannot prove it with brilliant theological reasoning; those who want to be saved and intend to give an eternal value to their lives; in other words, the entire Church, who never ceases to marvel at the gift of "God with us."

2. *We go to Bethlehem to find peace.* The angels proclaimed: "Glory to God in high heaven, and peace on earth." Peace has two components, one vertical, the other horizontal. The prophets, and in particular Isaiah, have indicated that this peace is the total realization of all Messianic good. This "Biblical" peace is our most cherished Christmas gift. It is the program of Christ's life (cf. Luke 2:14; John 20:19-20). This peace has its origin in the glory of God, and man will be able to live this peace only when he is enlightened by the glory of God. The divine Word empties Himself to fill us with His grace. He lowers Himself to lift us up. He becomes silent to teach us to speak with wisdom, weak to make us strong, small to help us grow, poor to free us of earthly goods. He becomes man to bring God near us, to give us His friendship, to have us regain our original happiness.

3. *To go to Christ is to go to the source of joy.* The angel said to the shepherds: "I proclaim tidings of great joy...a Savior has been born to you." All those who visited Bethlehem were filled with joy. St. Leo the Great said: "Today our Savior is born, let us rejoice. There is no room for sadness; life, which destroys the fear of

death, has come to fill us with the joy of the eternal promise.... Everyone can participate in this happiness. The reason for our common joy is the birth of Christ who frees all men by destroying sin and death. The honest man is happy because his reward is near. The sinner rejoices because his pardon has come. The unfaithful person takes courage because he is called to life. The Son of God has taken on our human nature in order to reconcile it with its Creator."

Pope Paul VI said: "God is our happiness, our joy and our delight. God is the fullness of life not only for Himself but also for us. God revealed Himself in love; He has satisfied our desires. God comprehends our shortcomings, our wickedness and our sins. God presents Himself to man as mercy, grace, salvation, as a wonderful and glorious surprise.... The message of the angel is intended also for us: You have nothing to fear! I come to proclaim good news to you—tidings of great joy to be shared by the whole people. Our religion is a religion of salvation, a religion of happiness. Joy is Christ's gift to the world" (Paul VI, Dec. 20, 1972).

HOLY FAMILY

Elderly People

Readings: Sirach 3:3-6, 12-14
Colossians 3:12-21
Matthew 2:13-15, 19-23

The Sunday after Christmas has always been dedicated to the family.

Following the suggestion of the First Reading, it may be good to dedicate a little time to the weaker and perhaps more forgotten members of the family. Elderly people have many problems, both material and spiritual. It is necessary to know these people, to appreciate and love them. Various factors such as age, a body that does not function as it should, a sense of uselessness, contribute to create a difficult psychological situation. It is important that elderly people do not give up in the battle of activity; even if they are not as precise and perfect as they used to be, they must do something.

Old people have more time to think and reflect, and they realize that they have made mistakes. The longer we live the more possibility we have to make mistakes; however, nothing good can be obtained by constant reference to these mistakes. And certainly throughout the long life of any person many things have been done well. There is much good which must not be forgotten.

It is necessary to appreciate old people. To reach old age is to reach the fullness of life. Old age is not an age like the others, nor is it an age after the others; it is a meeting with all ages. The elderly person can review his past and obtain a profound new outlook on life which is necessary for himself and useful to others. Frequently he can synthesize a problem almost intuitively. It is difficult for an old person to be deluded. He has experienced the vanity of passing things and knows the nobility of that which remains. In the eyes of a young person we see enthusiasm and fervor; in those of an old person we see wisdom and splendor. Henry Dominic Lacordaire once said: "The eyes of an old person express purity and tenderness, perfection and resemblance to the heavenly Father."

There is also much goodness in old age. Good things mellow with age. With age the energetic, impulsive or contradictory aspects of our character become calm, tender and cooperative. Our contact with God becomes more intimate as we grow old. The old person is nearer to the kingdom of the Father, in harmony with eternity; the light of resurrection and eternal life shines in his eyes. The old person is the best witness of Christian hope. He is already God's dwelling place.

Old people need love, affection and human warmth. By accepting them for what they are, with all their defects, we can give them the love they need. To love our old folks is nothing more than to give them what we have received from them. They give us an opportunity to develop our Christian and human capacity to love; so let there be joy in whatever we do for them.

To simply receive loving care and affection is not sufficient; passivity is not good. To keep alive is an obligation. To grow old is an art. Every art has norms to follow. Here are some for the art of growing old.

1. Do not expect too much from others. One of the secrets of happiness is spiritual independence. Egoism is part of the reality in which we live.

2. Do not get angry if things do not go well. Nothing should disturb our peace and calm. There is a lot of psychological wisdom in the expression: "Keep smiling." To mature, to grow old, is a law of life; in a certain sense, it is the goal of life. Diogenes had a ready answer for those who asked his age: "I don't worry about it, no one can steal my years!" We are as old as we feel.

3. The best way to live the solitude of old age is to keep active. To have something to do, something to accomplish, is to have a reason to live. Just because one is old does not mean he is useless. History is full of examples. Giuseppe Verdi was 80 when he composed "Falstaff." Michelangelo produced masterpieces up to his death at 89. Titian painted his famous self-portrait at 99. George Bernard Shaw continued writing until he was 94. Goethe completed "Faust" at 81. The Council of Trent was convoked by Pope Paul III when he was 78. Pope Leo XIII wrote his famous encyclical, *Rerum novarum*, at 81 and Pope John XXIII was 81 when he convoked Vatican II. True, we are not all geniuses but we can be well occupied. There were many books we wanted to read when we were young. Why not read them now? Perhaps in our younger days we did not have time to develop or strengthen friendships. Why not do so now?

4. As the body grows old it becomes weaker, slows down and does not always respond. To keep busy is fine

in theory but not always possible in practice. This is very true; however, the interior attitude is very important. The spirit lives with the body, and joy is one of the best medicines. It remains a fact that old age means suffering in spite of all the care and moral strength one might have. Suffering could become our spiritual friend in our twilight years. Christ's life can be divided into three periods: His hidden life, His apostolic life and His suffering. Our vocation as Christians begins with faith, is developed through works and is completed in suffering.

5. More than anything else, during our old age we should get to know God. As children our curiosity led us to the things of nature, our youth was full of human love, as adults we were concerned with social problems but in old age the idea of God and His infinite love become second nature to us. Our physical energy is less and therefore there is more room for the Holy Spirit. Loneliness, which is frequently part of old age, can be considered as an invitation to pass some time with the Lord. Death is at work in our bodies, but interiorly we can renew our life day by day (cf. 2 Corinthians 4:12-15).

PASTORAL REFLECTIONS

1. We were created for life and we must do everything possible to protect this life. Let us list *a few suggestions for happiness in old age.* Take a walk every day, and get sufficient sleep. Frequently lift your thoughts to God and confide your worries to Him. Be calm, orderly and patient in everything you do. Eat slowly, never completely satisfy your appetite, drink what is sufficient only to quench your thirst. Speak only when it is necessary, and then say only half of what you intended to say. Never forget that the others count on you, but you cannot count on them. Sadness, hatred and a sense of guilt are your worst enemies; keep them far away! Live in joy and peace: with yourself, with others and with God.

2. *Old age is the time to dialogue with God.* Separation from men should bring about a greater interest in God. Mental prayer more than verbal formula will nourish this silent friendship, which can be beneficial for others. When we were younger, others benefited materially from our efforts; now we can help them spiritually. Our prayers have a universal and ecumenical value.

3. *A prayer for old age.* Lord, teach me how to grow old! Help me to understand that if others are relieving me of responsibility, it is for the good of all concerned; if they do not ask my opinion, it is not because they are angry with me. Do away with my pride based on my long years of experience that no one is indispensable. As my activity and need of material things lessen, draw me closer to Yourself.

Lord, I want to be useful to others with my optimism, my courage and my prayers. I do not want to bemoan the good old days when.... I offer my daily suffering for the good of all mankind. I want to fade away in Your peace and joy!

JANUARY 1
SOLEMNITY OF THE MOTHER OF GOD

Mary: an Example for Meditation

Readings: Numbers 6:22-27
Galatians 4:4-7
Luke 2:16-21

Mary contemplated all that Jesus did (cf. Third Reading).

Life without meditation is like a plant without water, like a beautiful scenery without light. We need some time to separate facts from ideals, action from virtue, noise from truth. Meditation gives us an opportunity to know and appreciate God's values. It is wonderful to live, but to know how to live is even better. It is delightful to read, but to know how to read life is much more useful. Science is useful, but wisdom is our salvation. Only through meditation can we enter the supernatural world and begin to contact eternity. Our journey towards life begins when we can stop every now and then to verify our position.

If we are frequently with Christ, we will become "like Christ." Meditation transforms the Christian. The listener becomes a follower; the spark of love becomes a flame. Faith becomes decisive trust; hope becomes charity. Intimate conversation with God will not make everything perfectly clear. Strangely this does not discourage us; in fact, it increases our desire and our need to know God better. It increases our faith. Mary lived with Christ for more than thirty years. Certainly they frequently conversed together, and Mary "did not grasp what he said." However, she continued to model her life on what she learned from her Son.

Meditation has always been a part of those who live for God. In the Old Testament silence and meditation preceded every contact with God. Abraham is called to contemplate God's promises; Moses must present himself to God alone and remain on Mt. Sinai for forty days in meditation. Elias the prophet must walk in meditation for some time before he can meet God on Mt. Horeb. The chosen people wander in the desert for forty years to regain their intimacy with God. In the New Testament Christ gives us the example of meditation in silence, when He retreats to the desert for forty days. The Apostles followed this example. St. Paul nourishes himself in silent prayer for three years before beginning his tireless apostolic activities. Mary, Queen of the Apostles, received the Word of God throughout her entire life. The saints knew how to integrate meditation and contemplation in their active lives.

Passing from theory to practice, it will be useful to recall some of the basic norms for meditation. There is no doubt that the first requirement is silence. Pope Paul underlined the necessity of silence when he said: "To be able to understand our religion we need silence, interior and exterior silence. By silence we mean freedom from noise, from all the sense impressions coming from our surroundings which fill us with images. Whether we like it or not, these images, entering through the senses, slow down our thoughts and impede prayer. Silence does not mean sleep; it means conversation with ourselves, reflection, an attempt to regain our forces" (Paul VI, Dec. 5, 1973).

When one is in silence with men and things it is possible to enter into union with God. This union becomes the basis of our Christian lives, because without God's help we can do nothing on the supernatural level (cf. John 15:5). Our external position has a certain importance. Blaise Pascal once said: "Your external attitude should be one of prayer. Present yourself to God as if He were visible, and after a few minutes you will be absorbed in prayer and meditation."

Once we have acquired external and internal silence and asked God to assist us, we are ready to listen to the Word of God. Read slowly. It is not necessary to have an intellectual image of the whole passage. If there is little or no interior response, do not get frustrated, read on. The Word of God will not remain void (cf. Isaiah 55:11).

The Word of God is like a clear spring. To quench our thirst, it is not necessary to drink all the water in the spring; a small amount is sufficient. The intellectual activity is completed with an act of the will. Directly or indirectly, the reading will help us to reflect on God's words; this reflection is our reply to God. This reply becomes part of our way of life once the will accepts it. Frequently at this point of the meditation we spontaneously praise and converse with God, which indicates that we are in communication with Him. It is useful to end our meditation with a clear decision which will enlighten our day. Mary lived in constant union with God, because everything reminded her of God's infinite redemptive love.

It should be pointed out that besides preparation and theory, a certain part of the contact between man and God is mysterious and invisible. God cannot be placed in any category, nor can He be enclosed in our spiritual emotion. Even with the assistance of the Holy Spirit we can never concretely grasp His plan of action; He works where He wills (cf. John 3:8) and His groanings cannot be expressed in speech (cf. Romans 8:26).

Because of various circumstances our meditation can also be empty and in no way mystical. Family situations, anxiety and worry about human problems can interfere with our meditation.

We must have confidence in our dialogue with God, even if it seems empty; it can increase our humility. At the last moment we can transform everything into an act of love. Our sense of failure can increase our faith and trust in God's help. In the more difficult moments of our meditation we can always increase our faith, hope and charity which are the goal of contact with the Father. In one way or another we can always discover the face of God.

PASTORAL REFLECTIONS

1. The Church still recommends *the Spiritual Exercises* as a necessary period of spiritual reinforcement. A car needs to be "tuned up" every now and then; the soil needs periodic rest; man needs time to meditate if he wants to be an effective Christian. We will gather what we have sown. We will grow in proportion to what we have assimilated. What we have been able to elaborate in our hearts will be the measure of our maturity.

2. *Meditation is necessary for life.* Even before birth an infant learns to move. The heart beats, the head, the arms and legs, hands and feet all move; these move-

ments will be necessary for survival after birth. Our life on earth is a progress in the life of grace, a preparation for eternal life.

3. *Mary is our example and sure source of help* for our spiritual growth. "Mary is the supreme ideal of perfection; her beauty is the integration of human and divine beauty. She is full of grace, full of the Holy Spirit, full of splendor. Mary will fill us with the desire of spiritual renewal" (Paul VI, May 16, 1975).

SECOND SUNDAY AFTER CHRISTMAS

Creation and Elevation to the Supernatural

Readings: Sirach 24:1-4, 8-12
Ephesians 1:3-6, 15-18
John 1:1-18

Today's liturgy has us contemplate the overwhelming problem of sanctity. Everything God has done, from the creation to the manifestation of His glory, is part of a plan for man's sanctification.

The Book of Genesis is the beginning of Revelation; this indicates that the purpose of creation is the spiritual elevation of creatures. The fact that the chosen people cross the Red Sea is interpreted by Isaiah and Micah as a spiritual passage from the slavery of sin to the freedom of grace (cf. Isaiah 51:9-10; Micah 4:6-7). The Psalmist frequently begs to be freed from the deep waters and turbulent current, to enjoy the salvation of God (cf. Psalms 42:8; 65:10-12; 107:29; 124:1-4). The elevating potential of nature is very clear in the Books of Wisdom and Sirach; God's attributes are reflected in nature (cf. Wisdom 13:19; Sirach 17:8). The manifestation of God's goodness and the invitation to reach Him through nature is enthusiastically accepted by the seven sons of Maccabees who together with their mother were put to death by Antiochus (cf. 2 Maccabees 7:20-29).

The sacred dimension of creation is very explicit in the New Testament, where it is related to Christ, to salvation and to the final judgment. St. John and St. Paul interpret well the consecration of nature which came about through the birth and resurrection of Christ. In his letter to the Romans, Paul develops the idea that the knowledge of God's attributes will be through the created world which awaits the revelation of the sons of God (cf. Romans 8:19). In his letters to the Ephesians and Colossians Paul describes how nature is part of our sanctity and the glorification of Christ. He describes these truths with increasing enthusiasm, profound inspiration, exceptional intuition and synthesis. In fact, he has produced an indestructible treatise on religious cosmology or the theology of earthly reality.

In order to show the connection between nature and man's salvation, St. John gives a central position to the person and activity of the Son of God (cf. Third Reading). "In the beginning was the Word." John's choice of the word "beginning" is an evident reference to the first chapter of Genesis which speaks of creation. "Through him all things came into being"; "through" according to the original Greek preposition *dia* indicates a principal causality. In other words, the Word with the Father created everything that came into being, and apart from Him nothing came to be. This clearly eliminates the idea of two creative sources, the creation of good and the creation of evil. God alone created and Christ is the idea, the cause and the end of all creatures. John concludes that the purpose of creation is our sanctification; he passes spontaneously from the natural to the supernatural. He sees miracles as Christ's way of entering directly and intimately into communication with man. Christ has a full life; we can participate in this life through the sacrament of His humanity, and we are part of this humanity through the sacramentality of creation. This plan for man's sanctification is clear in nature; accepting this plan we become adopted children of God (cf. Third Reading).

PASTORAL REFLECTIONS

1. The Book of Wisdom tells us that *we should be able to perceive the presence of God in earthly reality.* The four seasons and the repeated renewal of nature in spring are clear indications of Providence and the divine goodness. The Christian should develop the ability to perceive the insistent love of God in all created things. Nature is full of signs for our sanctification.

2. The dynamic center of creation is Christ. Through Him *nature became the process of sanctification.* Some people use nature to exclude the supernatural; by doing so they ignore the very motivation of the cosmos. Cosmology cannot be non-religious; real humanism must be Christian.

3. The Logos produces *cosmic freedom* through His Word. If this Word is accepted, there is order in creation. If the message of Christ is not accepted, creation does not make sense. In order to keep our world beautiful, we must accept and live that Word who was the beginning of creation and will terminate all earthly activity. World ecology should be seen in the light of Christ.

THE EPIPHANY OF THE LORD

A Festivity of Light

Readings: Isaiah 60:1-6
Ephesians 3:2-3, 5-6
Matthew 2:1-12

In a certain sense the Epiphany concludes the Christmas period. Isaiah enjoys using the comparison between religion and light (cf. First Reading).

To worship the sun as the source of life is rather common in the history of man. Early Eastern people also considered the sun as being capable of inspiring good thoughts to man. Almost all religions use the concept of divine light. The history of the Hebrew people is frequently connected with light. A column of fire led the chosen people through the desert (cf. Exodus 13:21). God appeared to them in a luminous cloud (cf. Exodus 16:10) and as a consuming fire (cf. Exodus 24:17). God uses fire to show His power (cf. 1 Kings 18:19-46). The Old Testament considers God as being clothed in light (cf. Psalm 104:2). The Book of Wisdom considers light practically as a divine person.

Divine light reaches its fullness in the Incarnation: Christ is the light. St. Luke describes Him as the morning sun who will shine on those who sit in darkness (cf. Luke 1:78-79) and St. John frequently refers to Christ as light. The shepherds saw the Child surrounded by light, and the Magi were led to Christ by the light of a star. Another clear demonstration that Christ is the light is His transfiguration on Mt. Tabor. When He was crucified, darkness covered the earth, because the source of light was momentarily destroyed, and in His resurrection Christ regained His divine light. And when the story of salvation is completed, Christ will be there in all His glory as the light of the new creation (cf. Revelation 21:23).

It is interesting to consider some of the reasons why Christ is called the sun of the universe.

The sun bathes creation and fills it with life, yet we cannot get a hold of the sun. God became man and dynamically inserted Himself in our nature, yet He remains inaccessible (cf. 1 Timothy 6:16). There are many aspects to the comparison of Christ to the sun: both give their light gratuitously; nature cannot exchange the gift; in their giving they are neither consumed nor emptied. The sun continues to influence the earth even when it is hidden behind the clouds or during the night. Christ is the silent friend of all mankind even if He is not known, nor accepted, nor loved.

The fact that light is necessary for every type of life is another reason why God presents Himself as the light of the world. Scientific considerations might be superfluous, but they will help us enjoy this marvelous truth. Plants produce glucose by using sunlight, and glucose is the source of energy for all forms of life. Without sunlight there would be no food; even the fish, deep in the ocean, depend directly or indirectly on the glucose produced by microscopic marine plants. The energy obtained from coal and petroleum originally was light energy absorbed by plants millions of years ago. Much of the progress of present technology depends on the use and application of light in its various forms. Light reveals the marvels of creation. It takes some time to fully grasp the spiritual significance of Christ's declaration: "I am the light of the world" (John 8:12). He presents Himself in this way to help us understand that He has come to bring us life (cf. John 1:4; 12:35).

PASTORAL REFLECTIONS

1. Many artists have presented the birth of Christ as an invasion of light. *At Christmas the world is invaded with light; Christ is the light of the world.* The life of a Christian is to live and grow in this light in order to glow with its brilliance.

2. *Wisdom must be enlightened by Christ.* Tradition tells us that the Magi were learned men and yet they felt the need to know the Messiah. True science cannot remain within the realm of simple human research; it leads one to the boundaries of the eternal. Albert Einstein once said: "Science without religion is paralyzed." Only in Christ can research become full possession and restlessness be transformed into the peace and joy of light.

3. *Today's Liturgy invites us to be missionaries.* The Magi returned home full of light and joy; it is easy to imagine how they talked about what they had seen and heard. They are the first representatives of Christ's universal kingdom, an inevitable consequence of the light of Christ. "Men do not light a lamp and then put it under a basket, they set it on a stand where it gives light to all in the house" (Matthew 5:15). As Christians, it is our duty to spread the light of Christ which is the salvation of the world.

BAPTISM OF THE LORD

Baptism

Readings: Isaiah 42:1-4, 6-7
Acts 10:34-38
Matthew 3:13-17

Reading the account of Christ's baptism (cf. Third Reading) reminds us of our baptism.

Baptism is the foundation and most decisive act of our spiritual life. The promise of salvation through washing with water is frequent in the Old Testament. St. Peter sees the flood of Noah's time as prefiguring our salvation by the baptismal bath (cf. 1 Peter 3:20). St. Paul makes the same reflection on the passage through the Red Sea (cf. 1 Corinthians 10:1-2). The prophets speak clearly of purifying waters (cf. Zechariah 13:1; Ezekiel 36:24-28). Christ wants to be baptized by John to officially begin His public life, but moreso to inaugurate God's new people.

The first effect of Baptism is purification from sin. In the early Church, Baptism was by immersion which illustrates more clearly the washing. It also symbolized a burial of the old covenant to make room for our new life in Christ.

Through Baptism there is a new birth (cf. John 3:5), a new creature (cf. 2 Corinthians 5:17), the adopted son of God is born. Baptism places us in contact with the Trinity and with the entire Church (cf. Second Reading). Faith and Baptism are the means of salvation and Christ intends that they be together (cf. Matthew 28:19). The basis of dialogue with God is faith and Baptism. God gives Himself to us in charity, and in Baptism we respond with our faith. Baptism is the peak of our life with the Trinity which is a free gift; we do not merit it, nor do we have a right to it.

There has always been much discussion about the Baptism of small children. It seems that the Father is impatient; He wants these small creatures to be His adopted children as soon as possible. It is the love of the Son which wants to apply the fruits of Redemption without delay, and the Holy Spirit desires to act in them immediately. The Church rejoices, embracing these children. They are the object of that motherly love of the Church. They are the growth of the Church. A mother does not wait until her children are grown to express and manifest her love and affection for them.

Through Baptism the seed of a new life is planted in the small child. There is a normal development for all types of life: the seed, birth, progress, maturity and reproduction. The small child is the fertile soil where this process towards maturity begins. This, however, does not explain the problem of the acceptance and cooperation necessary to reach maturity in the life of Christ. St. Augustine answered this objection by saying: "The child does not have a conscious faith; he believes by vocation" (Letter 98:10). At first others accept and cooperate for the small child. The family takes the responsibility for the progress and development of the child's new life in Christ. The Church formally delegates this responsibility to the godparents whose first duty is to foster the spiritual growth by their example. Baptism of a newborn child is not intended to be just another ceremony, it means being involved in the development of Christ's kingdom in the world. This becomes possible when the family and the parish are united in prayer and action.

PASTORAL REFLECTIONS

1. *We must be thankful.* It is necessary to express our gratitude for our new life as adopted children of God. "Life would be useless if there were not the possibility of rebirth through Baptism to the supernatural life" (Paul VI, March 29, 1975).

2. *Faith must be part of our lives.* "When we were carried to the door of the Church we were asked: 'What do you want from the Church?' and the reply was, 'I want

faith.' An extremely simple dialogue, yet very important; faith is the key to Christian salvation. The faith we seek in Baptism is not so much a formed faith but an attitude, a disposition, which will guide and enlighten us in our lives as Christians..." (Paul VI, April 24, 1974).

3. *Faith also means to trust the Church.* Baptism establishes a relationship between us and the Church which is both visible and mysterious, historic and eschatological. The Church is the Mystical Body of Christ; we should be happy and proud to be members. We must learn how to love the Church. Rosmini once said: "We cannot love the Church of Christ too much."

FIRST SUNDAY OF LENT

The Origin of Mankind and Sin

Readings: Genesis 2:7-9; 3:1-7
Romans 5:12-19
Matthew 4:1-11

Something went wrong at the beginning of man's existence and this altered his original relationship with God. Man declined rapidly from his original state of primal perfection to an existence without morals. Paul Tournier, a well-known Swiss psychologist, once said: "It was not the animal who progressively became man, but it was man who regressed towards the animal." The Bible mentions the initial difficulty man had in his contact with God. Using a style adapted to simple, Oriental people, the Book of Genesis clearly indicates that something went wrong (cf. Genesis 8:21). Just what happened, how and when is not clear. The first books of the Bible are historical and simply relate events. It is up to the theologians to discuss the facts and how they came about. The author of Genesis frequently repeats himself and uses many particular details. This is his way of stressing the importance of his message; namely, something happened, and the alliance between God and man was broken, and man is responsible for it. This is reconfirmed in the Book of Sirach which was written about two centuries before the birth of Christ (cf. Sirach 25:24). Later St. Paul will develop the universal consequences of this unfortunate event which is related to man's origin (cf. Romans 1; 2; 4; 7). Following God's inspiration, the Church has always taught the reality of sin at man's origin. Vatican II frequently mentions the fact that man set himself against God from the very beginning of his existence (cf. Pastoral Constitution on the Church in the Modern World, no. 13; Decree on the Instruments of Social Communication, no. 7). This unhappy event is often referred to in the Church's teaching to better appreciate God's marvelous plan of Redemption. Many aspects of the doctrine of original sin are not clear, but as Pascal once said: "If we eliminate this mysterious event, then the histories of man and of the Church become mysterious." "To refuse the doctrine on original sin is more a sin than not to believe in God, because by eliminating original sin we do away with Christ our Savior" (Bernanos).

Reflection on the nature and transmission of original sin can be useful. The nature is in the relation between God and man. Urged by the Evil One, man wanted "to know good and evil"; that is, he wanted to become God. He wanted to become the principle of life and law. Together with an abuse of his liberty, man despised God as if God offended man's rights. In fact, the Evil One suggested that if God made laws for man it was because He had to protect His position which belonged to man by right of his nature. God's generosity is considered as a way to cheat man out of his divine rights. This is the most tragic aspect of the rebellion: it is a sin against the goodness and truth of God. Formal disobedience is simply the conclusion and manifestation of man's internal mistrust.

Man set himself against God, separated himself from the "tree of life," and the consequences were decisive and disastrous. Separation from God brings about a psychological and social breakdown in man. Adam and Eve become aware of their limits, of their moral poverty, and they flee from God because they can no longer accept His love. God accepts man's rebellion and suspends His intimate relationship with man. Man lost his friendship with God. Now he must toil for his bread, while she suffers in childbirth. Both fear the pain and mystery of death. Man's relations with his fellowmen are also disturbed. Adam and Eve begin to cast blame upon each other. This division becomes social in their children: Cain kills Abel (cf. Genesis 4:8); Lamech also kills in senseless violence (cf. Genesis 4:24). In a burst of pride against God, man builds the tower of Babel: it ends in a disastrous problem of communication (cf. Genesis 11). After man's initial separation from God the history of sin grows as man drifts farther and farther from his Creator. In a certain sense it seems that man has been entrusted to the Evil One to be tortured (cf. Luke 13:16).

Man offended God's goodness; nevertheless, God will find a way to reconcile man and overcome evil. At the very moment of the separation God promised to give man another chance (cf. Genesis 3:15), and His promise was followed by action. God frees Adam from his guilt (cf. Wisdom 10:1). After the flood He makes a new agreement with Noah (cf. Genesis 8:15; 9:17). For His new people He chooses Abraham and Sarah (cf. Genesis 21). Finally using Moses, Aaron and Miriam, He frees His people from slavery in Egypt in view of a covenant with all mankind. It is already quite clear that, through the future Messiah, man will be able to be God's friend again (cf. Second Reading).

PASTORAL REFLECTIONS

1. The tragedy of original sin should convince us of *the existence and power of the devil*. It would be contrary to the Bible to deny the existence of the Evil One. The Book of Genesis describes him as "the serpent," which Oriental people consider as a divinity. The Book of Wisdom refers to the demon as the one who divides or the one who disturbs (cf. Wisdom 2:24). The New Testament has various names for the Evil One according to what he does: the devil, the serpent, the liar, the dragon,

Beelzebul, Satan. The Church with her sacramental liturgy is "the Woman" who constantly opposes the forces of evil, and we are the battleground where the forces of good and evil contend.

2. *The power of the demon is not infinite* nor is it beyond our strength (cf. 1 Corinthians 10:13). United to Christ we can overcome the devil; however, it is a constant battle (cf. Romans 16:20). If at times we weaken and give up, the mercy and forgiveness of Jesus are always available (cf. Romans 5:20). He has offered Himself to free us from sin (cf. 2 Corinthians 5:21). Considering the consequences of man's original behavior, we must not lose sight of the marvelous plan of salvation realized by Christ.

3. *Supernatural rebirth becomes easy if we let Mary help us.* The first promise to re-establish friendship with God is in the figure of the Woman who will crush the head of the serpent (cf. Genesis 3:15). The Virgin Mary is present at the moment the plan of salvation becomes a reality when she says to the angel: "Let it be done to me according to your word" (Luke 1:38). She is the first one to reveal our salvation when she shows the Child Jesus to the shepherds and the Magi. She is present when Christ begins His apostolate at Cana. She is present on Calvary where our salvation is completed. She is also present at Pentecost, the beginning of the Church. Mary has given us an example and an invitation to keep her present.

SECOND SUNDAY OF LENT

Faith: Risks and Promises

Readings: Genesis 12:1-4
2 Timothy 1:8-10
Matthew 17:1-9

Abram's departure towards the unknown (cf. First Reading) gives us an excellent opportunity to consider the risks and promises of faith.

The journey of faith has two ends: man's finite reality and God's infinite perfection. On earth we can fully believe in God, but we cannot fully possess Him. Our first difficulty in faith stems from our functional inability to see God as He is. To believe is to walk towards the unknown as Abram did or to climb Mt. Tabor as the Apostles did (cf. Third Reading). We can progress and mature in knowledge of God, but He will always remain inaccessible and ineffable. According to St. Augustine, "Once we have found God we still have everything to discover." As long as we live in time we will never be satisfied with our relation with God. The more we know about God, the more there is to know and the more we want to know. "Now we see in a mirror dimly" (1 Corinthians 13:12). Job expresses the same idea when he says "Lo, he passes by me, and I see him not; he moves on but I do not perceive him" (Job 9:11). God told Moses: "Then I will take away my hand, and you shall see my back; but my face shall not be seen" (cf. Exodus 33:23).

Departure implies leaving something. Abram left his country, his possessions and his family. The three Apostles on Mt. Tabor left the people and the other Apostles. To live our faith means to leave, to be separated from those who do not believe. There are two ways to look at the world: historically and prophetically. History is based on man, prophecy on a supernatural ideal. History is man's way of looking at things, man's action; prophecy is God's outlook, the action of His love. History is a science. Prophecy is wisdom. It is evident that there is a clear separation between those who believe and those who do not believe. Every separation is difficult, for we do not like to leave things behind (cf. 1 John 2:15-17).

Separation is not easy, nor is it simple to live for a promise which in reality is invisible. Abram is an excellent example. Through faith he obeyed God's command: "Go forth from the land of your kinsfolk and from your father's house to a land that I will show you." He had no idea where he was being directed (cf. Genesis 12:1).

Faith means to leave the certitude of reality and embrace the unknown, to put aside earthly ideas and accept the thoughts and ways of God. The Christian embarks on a spiritual journey, nourished and supported only by the Word of God.

At times the hardships of this journey become very intense, almost unbearable. The Apostles were so enthusiastic about what they saw on Mt. Tabor that they wanted to set up three tents and stay for a while. Then all of a sudden everything disappeared and all they saw was Jesus. There are moments in our life of faith when everything goes well. We are enthusiastic and quite sure of what we want to do. Then all of a sudden, it all disappears. The monotony of everyday life overwhelms us. Our minds are tormented by doubts; our will becomes sluggish. We feel lonely and want to return to what we left behind. This is the moment of faith. These ups and downs make us realize just how small we are and urge us to believe more firmly in God's goodness which is always present, even if not apparent in the events of everyday life.

To have a more complete idea of faith we should include another concept. For a full and loving reply to the divine indications we need trust. Love involves suffering, and trust involves trial. In the moment of trial, faith becomes trust. The Bible gives us many examples: Abram is the father and model of those who believe precisely because his faith was tested (cf. Wisdom 3:5; Sirach 44:20). Moses' faith was tried, he was sure that God would fulfill His promises, but at times he was about to give in to the insistence of his people and abandon God. In spite of his moments of weakness and trial (cf. Numbers 20:1-12) Moses did not lose faith; he trusted (cf. Hebrews 11:23-29). The history of the Hebrew people is a history of trial and suffering, which transforms faith into trust. Their prolonged wandering through the desert increased their trust in God. Even after they reached the promised land there were trials: Jerusalem was occupied by pagans; there was slavery and persecution. Through these negative events, their faith became total trust in God who remained faithful to His promises (cf. Isaiah 30:15). The life of Job gives us the best example of the interdependence of faith and trust in trial. Job shows us how faith can grow through suffering until it becomes complete trust.

The New Testament is even more explicit in showing that faith must also be trust. St. John the Baptist, the Apostles and Mary are clear models of God's new people who live their faith through a dedicated trust. True Christianity is centered on the reality and apparent folly of the cross.

PASTORAL REFLECTIONS

1. *Our faith must be constantly nourished by the Word of God* (cf. Romans 10:14-18). The Scriptures should be part of our everyday life. To thoroughly appreciate the abundance and intensity of a rainfall one must stand in the rain and be soaked to the skin. The saints were saturated with the Word of God which enabled them to overcome the difficulties of a life of faith. They perfected their faith by accepting the teaching of the Church, encouraged by the words of Christ: "He who hears you, hears me" (Luke 10:16). When we approach the Word of God, we should not consider it to be an intellectual exercise, nor try to find the solution to social or political problems. The Scriptures will nourish our faith and transform it into trust in the Lord. There is a lot of truth in what Francis Fenelon, Archbishop of Cambri, once said: "The less we try to reason, the more reasonable we become."

2. *We come to know Christ in the Bible.* St. Jerome said that ignorance of the Scriptures is ignorance of Christ. If we transcribe the Scriptures in our hearts, they will lead us to Christ. God has spoken through His Son, and we must listen to Him. "We should learn the marvelous teaching of Christ. Our inability to understand the connection between life and religion will be enlightened by His superior wisdom" (Paul VI, April 16, 1975).

3. *There is a great need for strong faith.* "The time has come to evaluate our acceptance of Christ. Our thoughts and actions could conflict with the Gospels and our salvation. We must have a very clear and complete idea of our values, which are absolute and which are subordinate. We must decide the real purpose of our existence. Do we want to be authentic followers of Christ or simply another number on the baptismal record? Do we want God and Christ to be the center of our lives, or will everything we do depend on our egoism? It is unthinkable that a Christian be indifferent, uninterested, without energy or a sense of sacrifice. By definition, a Christian is a strong person. His faith must become a trust" (Paul VI, May 15, 1973 and August 18, 1974).

THIRD SUNDAY OF LENT

> Readings: Exodus 17:3-7
> Romans 5:1-2, 5-8
> John 4:5-42

Grace

In the First Reading of today's liturgy we see Moses produce water in abundance from a rock; in the Third Reading we hear the dialogue between Jesus and the Samaritan woman about the water of life. Water offers us an excellent comparison to contemplate the marvels of grace.

Perhaps the best way to appreciate water is to imagine ourselves lost in the middle of a desert without water. It is part of the culture of the people who live in the deserts to venerate water. A river or a spring for these people is a source of joy and festivity. It was a custom for the ancient Persians to meditate and rejoice along the banks of a river.

Grace is a mysterious reality. We never know just where or how much water is hidden in the earth. Grace is God's life communicated to man; this divine and infinite reality can never be completely known or understood by our limited minds. We can evaluate grace qualitatively, that is, we can be aware of its presence but cannot measure its essence.

Water within the earth appears here and there as a spring or an oasis. Man comes to know about it through its effects. In the history of man and of the Church, the manifestations of grace are mysterious. Frequently the wonderful fruits of grace appear where one would least expect them. There is a qualitative change in the Samaritan woman (cf. Third Reading), in Mary Magdalen, in Saul on the road to Damascus. Did anyone expect the almost unbelievable change in Francis of Assisi or in Ignatius of Loyola? God is free to act where He will; He alone is the sole author of every grace.

Water can transform the desert into a garden of every type of life. The essential effect of grace is the new interior life, which in turn brings about the qualitative change in man. Water can change its form: snow, vapor, ice. Man, too, can change not only from his primitive state to his present more advanced state always within his essence. Man can go beyond the limits of the finite and participate in the supernatural world of the infinite through grace, a free gift from God. Only in this way does man fully realize his personality. To be a philanthropist or a well-educated person is not sufficient; God's plan is that man become His adopted son through grace. God alone is the author of grace.

Alone Moses could do very little; with the grace of God he obtained water from a rock. The Samaritan woman was able to draw water from the well; Christ gave her the water of life. Grace is a totally gratuitous gift. Christ came into the world to give us the life of His grace. The prophets foretold His coming as an invasion of water that would renew the earth (cf. Ezekiel 36:25) and as "the source of living water" (cf. Jeremiah 2:13). Jesus, referring to the prophets, presents himself as the font of water and the new spirit which would purify and sanctify man (cf. John 7:38). Christ referred to Himself as "the river of life-giving water, clear as crystal" (cf. Revelation 22:1) and as the "spiritual rock" (cf. 1 Corinthians 10:4) from which life and holiness flow.

PASTORAL REFLECTIONS

1. *God waits for us to respond to His love.* Let us imagine the sorrow of a mother who has prepared all sorts of good things for her children and one of them, even though he is hungry, refuses to eat. God is not pleased when we fail to respond to His friendship. God created the entire universe in order to establish a covenant of life with us. It is not difficult to understand the invitation of St. Paul when he encourages us to participate in the life and grace that Christ brought. In fact, this is the essence of a Christian's life (cf. Second Reading).

2. *We continue to receive grace through Christ.* The Church is the "house of grace." Christ is present in the Church to distribute the waters of grace, to lead man to the source of life (cf. Revelation 7:17). Christ said: "I am the way, the truth and the life." St. Augustine, commenting on this passage, said: "He has always been the truth and the life but through the Incarnation He remains in the Church as the way to the truth and life of grace."

3. *Grace makes us apostles.* There is a particular detail in John's account of the dialogue between Jesus and the Samaritan woman which reveals the immediate change in her, namely: "The woman then left her water jar and went off into the town. She said to the people: 'Come and see someone who has told me everything I ever did!' " (cf. Third Reading). She became an apostle. Only grace, that is, vital contact with God, can produce this type of interior metamorphosis, this apostolic courage, this desire to witness to Christ.

FOURTH SUNDAY OF LENT

The Pedagogy of Faith

Readings: 1 Samuel 16:1, 6-7, 10-13
Ephesians 5:8-14
John 9:1-41

St. John's account of the man born blind is a masterpiece of signs and details. A very animated discussion takes place in which the question, "How could a man born blind see?" is probed.

The Pharisees argue from a negative point of view: Jesus does not keep the law of the Sabbath and is, therefore, a sinner, and, consequently, could not possibly work a miracle. This man was born blind, which indicates that he, too, is a sinner and must not be taken seriously. No one knows who this Jesus is, nor where He comes from. The man who was blind answers the negative arguments of the Pharisees, beginning with the simple fact that he was blind and now he sees. The man who brought about this change cannot be a sinner, since God does not hear the requests of a sinner; therefore, He must be a friend of God. Using good common sense the blind man reveals the jealousy of the Pharisees, and they become so irritated that they throw him out.

This miracle is full of meaning for us; it is an excellent lesson on the necessity, beauty and pedagogy of faith.

If we are to give a valid meaning to our existence, we can do so only through faith. Walking was very difficult for the blind man, because he had been blind. Life without faith is paralyzed; it has no purpose. The lack of faith separates man from nature and divides him from his fellowmen. Men are divided into many categories: strong and weak, young and old, honest and dishonest, rich and poor, modern and old-fashioned. Faith is the criterion to divide men interiorly. Those who witnessed the miracle were divided, some believed in Christ; others did not. This is why St. John frequently points out that the real battle is between light and darkness, between Christ and untruth.

This account is a very clear lesson in Christian faith. First the blind man listens to Jesus. He allows Jesus to touch him. He obeys by going to the pool of Siloam to wash. Surely Jesus cast light upon each of these acts to draw this man close to Himself. Grace worked immediately and abundantly in this man since he was open and sincere, free of complexes and prejudices. Shortly after the miracle Jesus invites this man to make an act of faith. It is spontaneous for him to reply: " 'I do believe, Lord,' and he bowed down to worship him" (cf. Third Reading). This man born blind begins with simple confidence and shortly after adores Christ as God. This is the pedagogical dimension of faith.

First, the word of Christ is a term of reference. Like a mirror, it shows us just what we are and what we should be. Like a sword, it penetrates and divides our very being. If the word finds us in an erroneous position, it can heal us, cleanse us and give us a new life (cf. John 15:3). By accepting this word, we are in contact with Christ. We are assimilated by Him. We become part of His life. The word of Christ is not simply literature; it is a Person: "I am the Truth."

There are two aspects to faith: it is an objective truth unchangeable in the Person of Christ, and it is a subjective truth changeable and progressive in man. Faith is constant and always new.

Through faith we can appreciate nature. Much of the joy of the man born blind came from the fact that he could now see the beauty and harmony of created things. The light of the sun enriches everything it illuminates; in the light of faith our cosmos becomes almost a beatitude. Nature without the light of faith is like a panorama seen through a pair of binoculars turned the wrong way.

Faith can give us happiness of life. Faith opens our intellects to supernatural ideals. It is the answer to our problems; it satisfies our most profound desires. Faith gives a purpose to our lives even if the fatigue remains. Faith is interior enthusiasm, because it is vital communication with God—that God whom one day we will see "face to face." What we see is beautiful, what we know is even more beautiful, but the beauty of what we believe surpasses everything else.

PASTORAL REFLECTIONS

1. *The just man lives by faith.* This is the constant message of the Scriptures (cf. Habakkuk 2:4; Romans 1:17; Galatians 2:11; Hebrews 9:38). The entire life of a Christian is full of faith, as all creation is flooded with the light of the sun. Faith in the small child is the poetry of innocence. As the child grows, faith enables him to accept the difficulties of his Christian life. In the doubts of the adolescent, faith establishes a personal contact with Christ. The young person feels the need to manifest the social dimension of his faith. For the adult, faith becomes the light for a more profound spiritual insight. Faith is that light shining in the eyes of an elderly person which enlightens the final stage of his earthly journey towards the Lord.

2. *Faith for the Christian has a name: Jesus Christ.* To believe in God is equivalent to believe in Jesus (cf. John 12:44; 14:1). Dostoevski once said: "If I were to meet truth and Jesus Christ, I would choose Jesus Christ." The world today has its masters of doubt, who try to undermine our faith with their new hypotheses. At times they use the Scripture, like the Pharisees did, to support their material outlook. The Christian is strong in his faith because he acknowledges Jesus Christ and knows how to put the other spirits to a test (cf. 1 John 4:1-6).

3. If the only title of the Church were *"fortress of faith,"* this would be sufficient to render it acceptable.

Externally many things can change. The Church can be considered outdated, but one fact remains: through the ages only the Church has offered certain truth to guide us along our earthly journey.

FIFTH SUNDAY OF LENT

The Resurrection of the Body

Readings: Ezekiel 37:12-14
Romans 8:8-11
John 11:1-45

We are living in a curious period of history. Science is advancing so rapidly that huge electronic brains are needed to remember everything man knows and yet there is so much ignorance about the final goal of life. The Scriptures and the liturgy have always made every effort to correct this earthly shortsightedness. "Without Christ, we cannot know what life is, nor what death is; without His doctrine, the history of man is meaningless; without His doctrine, we cannot even understand ourselves" (Pascal).

The resurrection of Lazarus (cf. Third Reading) gives us the possibility to review and, if necessary, revive our ideas about the resurrection of the body.

All the great religions have a special cult for the body of the deceased. Christian Revelation gives us a theology of the body. Contrary to stoic philosophy, the Old Testament teaches us to respect our bodies. After death there still remains a relationship between body and soul. Burial is a momentary separation, yet the body will reawaken (cf. 1 Samuel 2:6; Deuteronomy 32:39).

The prophets spoke of the resurrection of the body. They longed for it; Ezekiel mentions the resurrection of dried bones (cf. Ezekiel 37:1-14). Isaiah says we will drink with the Lord (cf. Isaiah 51:17). He also says that God will reward the just by prolonging their days (cf.

Isaiah 53:10). This concept is developed in the Book of Wisdom to the point where the glorification of the body becomes part of Jewish belief. Daniel the prophet gives us a clear idea: "Many of those who sleep in the dust of the earth shall awake, some to everlasting life, and some to shame and everlasting contempt" (Daniel 12:2). At the time of Christ the idea of the resurrection of the body was widespread. Perhaps only the Sadducees did not accept it. Christ not only reconfirms the indications of the Old Testament, but He restores life to the dead: the daughter of Jairus (cf. Mark 5:21), the son of the widow of Naim (cf. Luke 7:11-17), and His friend Lazarus (cf. Third Reading). There can be no doubts about our resurrection.

The teaching of the early Church considered the resurrection of Christ as an indisputable sign of His power and dominion over nature (cf. Acts 2:25-32; 4:11). Saint Paul developed the idea that Christ, risen from the dead, is the foundation of those who will repossess their bodies. Early Greek philosophy taught that after death the soul went to the kingdom of the immortals and the body was destroyed forever. Paul announced and defended the absolute unity of the human person and our eventual total resurrection, body and soul (cf. 1 Corinthians 15:12-20; Romans 8:23). St John spoke of the resurrection of our bodies (cf. John 5:28), and he exulted with those who die and rise in Christ (cf. Revelation 20:11-15). The guarantee that our bodies will rise is the power of Christ, the "Lord of glory" (cf. 1 Corinthians 2:8), the "author of salvation" (cf. Acts 3:6) who has said: "I am the resurrection and the life. Whoever believes in me, though he should die, will come to life" (cf. Third Reading).

We, too, will rise. "Our faith tells us we will rise. Our God is not a God of the dead but the God of the living" (Paul VI, Nov. 4, 1973).

PASTORAL REFLECTIONS

1. If we are candidates for eternal glorification, then it is not difficult to admit that *our bodies have a right to a profound and religious respect.*

First, social structure is undermined; next, ideas and ideals are shattered, and then life itself is despised. A few statistics will show that there is little respect for life. Each year about three million people attempt suicide; across the world each day about ten thousand people die in road accidents and some thirty thousand are injured. Besides the accidents and disasters, there are the wars; since 1945 there have been about fifty wars. If we add sickness and damage to health due to exaggeration and carelessness (alcohol, drugs, lack of sleep, etc.), we can have a good idea of how the human body is slaughtered. We should act differently if we remember that our body is a candidate for resurrection and eternal glorification.

2. *We should not be afraid of death.* In a letter to his sister, Mozart wrote: "Since death is the goal of our lives, I want to know this friend of man, not to be frightened but to be reassured. I never go to sleep without thinking that I might not wake up in the morning. By meditating on death, I have found the key to life and to a certain happiness." A motto for life could be the following: "Do everything as if you were to live forever; but do it well, as if you were to die tomorrow."

3. *For Christianity death is the door of hope.* The Christian is born, grows and dies, to live. Death is the moment when we pass from the state of mobile, imperfect life to the new state of complete perfection. Through death we leave ourselves and enter God, the goal of our lives and the principle of our glorification. Those who do not have this hope are already dead in this life, and this can explain their absurd ways. Those who live this hope enjoy life because they anticipate the joy of the life to come.

PASSION SUNDAY (PALM SUNDAY)

The Passion of Our Lord

Readings: Isaiah 50:4-7
Philippians 2:6-11
Matthew 26:14—27:66

A rapid glance at the history of the various civilizations shows us that man has always tried to express his relation with God through sacrifice. The purpose of sacrifice was to adore God, to thank Him for creation, to appease Him and, most important of all, to establish a spiritual contact with God in an alliance of friendship and mutual trust.

There is a certain development in the sacrificial rites of the Hebrew people. Their earliest sacrificial rites were characteristic of their nomadic life: they set up local altars, offered the fruits of the earth and invoked God spontaneously. The priest usually was the head of the family or the head of the tribe. Later, when they reached the promised land, their various sacrificial rites were performed in the temple of Jerusalem. This led to the necessity to codify the rules concerning sacrifices; the Book of Leviticus is a guide for the various types of sacrifice. With time they lost sight of the fundamental purpose of their sacrifices, the adoration of God, and an exasperating legalism and conformism set in, which was condemned by the prophets.

The doctrine of sacrifice in the New Testament completes that of the Old Testament; there is, however, a qualitative difference. The Letter to the Hebrews contains a good comparison between the two economies. In the Old Law the priest and victim are separate; in the New Law, Christ is both Priest and Victim. The expiatory offering of the Old Law could not be immolated because it contained sin; Christ is innocent, and He is sacrificed because He has assumed the sins of the world (cf. Hebrews 7:11; 8:6). According to the norms in Leviticus, the victim was predetermined and obligatory; Christ freely, lovingly, chooses to sacrifice Himself. The sacrifices in the Old Economy were temporal and repeated; in the New Economy it is always the same sacrifice of Christ which is applied to us. In the Old Liturgy the temple was the place of sacrifice; in the New it is wherever the Eucharist is celebrated. In the Old Testament the blood of animals purified; in the New it is the blood of God. The old sacrifices were to establish or reconfirm a covenant with God; Christ's sacrifice is the means for humanity to become the family of God. Only the sacrifice of Christ is perfect in every aspect. The author of the Book of Revelation presents Christ as the perfect Lamb sacrificed for humanity.

The Liturgy of Palm Sunday invites us to reflect on the Passion of Christ, the perfect sacrifice, which brought about our salvation.

PASTORAL REFLECTIONS

1. Referring to the three periods of the liturgical development of sacrifice in the Old Testament, there are three reflections for those who wish to enjoy the liturgical riches of the New Testament. *The Christian can have a private and personal liturgy* as the early Hebrews did. St. Peter tells us: "You too are...a holy priesthood, to offer spiritual sacrifices acceptable to God through Jesus Christ" (1 Peter 2:5). St. Paul invites us to do whatever we do for the glory of God (cf. 1 Corinthians 10:31).

2. Our personal and private liturgy is more effective when connected to the *Liturgy of the Church*. Why is the official liturgy of the Church a communitarian act? There are a number of reasons. It is the will of Christ. The liturgical community is the Mystical Body of Christ. The Eucharist—breaking bread together—presupposes a community. The liturgy of the Spouse of Christ in the Church is a sign and anticipation of the liturgy of the

kingdom of God. Being together in the liturgical community we know that Christ is with us as our Truth, Life and Way.

3. *Jesus must be the center of the liturgy.* There are various attitudes towards the entry of Jesus in our lives: indifference, hostility, or enthusiasm. When Jesus entered Jerusalem, young people and children were the most enthusiastic. They improvised the festivities even though the atmosphere was not favorable and they shouted with joy: "Blessed is He who comes in the name of the Lord!"

EASTER SUNDAY

The Resurrection of Our Lord

Readings: Acts 10:34, 37-43
1 Corinthians 5:6-8
John 20:1-9

By nightfall of Good Friday it seemed that everything had come to an end. The Apostles saw their Master covered with blood, crucified and buried. Messianic hope seemed to be buried, and the prophecies which proclaimed Him the "Son of God" now sounded empty. But Christ is the Lord of life and death and, on the third day, as He had promised, He rose from the dead.

The Resurrection of Christ changed the history of man. Man's values are now seen in a new light. Christ has become the criterion to identify man. With Him there is peace and universal brotherhood; without Him there is violence, division, strife and war. There are those who believe in eternal life and those who seek an earthly kingdom. There are those who make love of God and of neighbor the supreme rule of their individual and social lives and those who place force and revolution before everything. There are those who, through faith, have obtained truth and are, consequently, free and those who force their various opinions on others, violating their consciences. There are two ways of looking at the world and its history, and the conflict between them is evident (cf. Paul VI, April 11, 1976).

The guarantee and power of victory of life over death, of the glorious over the sinful, is the resurrection of Jesus. The large stone rolled across the opening of the grave was to put an end to everything; instead, it is the cornerstone of Christ's kingdom on earth. The Old Law is buried forever. The history of new creatures has begun, new works, new words, new hearts; love has overcome evil. The Christian is so certain of this, and so happy about it that he wants to share it with others to have them participate in his faith and joy (cf. Paul VI, April 18, 1976).

The primitive Church gave the name "Kyrios" to Jesus risen from the dead. For them it meant the Lord of lords, who would change the history of man.

Easter is principally the feast of the Church. Pope Leo the Great once said: "That which was first visible in the Redeemer, after the resurrection and ascension, has passed to the Church, the glorious Mystical Body of Christ. The vision and the light of Christ is replaced by the teachings of the Church, and His person by her representatives."

Christ saves mankind and gives life to the Church through those who believed in Him. The light and glory of Christ risen from the dead shines on and through every aspect of Christian life. St. Paul tells us: "Christ rose from the dead so that we could live a new life in him." What is this new life? One of the first things the risen Savior did was to give us the Holy Spirit, to forgive our sins and regain peace. It does not require profound psychological knowledge to see the connection between sin and sadness and between grace and happiness. The simple and marvelous greeting, "Peace be with you," will become a reality in our life if we do away with indifference, hatred, prejudice and egoism, making room for Christ in our lives. This certainly requires faith. The "good news" of the Gospels is faith-happiness. Total happiness is beatitude, and Jesus frequently uses this expression. "Blest are you, Peter, because my Father has revealed these things to you." "Blest are those who believe and accept the word of God." Elizabeth tells Mary she is blest because she has believed. Jesus had us in mind when He said to Thomas: "Blessed are those who have not seen and yet believe" (John 20:29).

PASTORAL REFLECTIONS

1. Easter offers us an occasion to *reconsider our commitment to the apostolate.* Easter Liturgy is so full of supernatural good news that it is spontaneous to want to share it with others. That small flame we held during the Liturgy of the Vigil helps us to rediscover our Redemption and invites us to illuminate others. The true Christian is a flaming torch, a living example, a herald of the new life. Our duty is to make a new world; the means necessary to do so are available. Quality is more important than number. The salvation of the world depends on those who have seen and heard Christ risen from the dead.

2. *Today everyone should rejoice.* "Peace and joy to all! Enjoy this wonderful day! Today our churches are full of song and happiness. Come and see, perhaps our religious experience will enlighten you. Come, you who are tired and oppressed, Christ will relieve you! Shout with joy to the entire world: Christ is risen, He is alive, He lives with us! This is our happiness, our victory. This is our salvation, not contained in hope but based on the reality of Christ's Resurrection and guaranteed by the truth of His word" (Paul VI, April 14, 1974; April 2, 1975).

3. *A Prayer.*

Lord, if You are with me, nothing frightens me: I am safe with You.

If You are near me, I do not fear the enemy: fight and speak with me.

If You guide me, I will not go astray: You are my way.

If You enlighten me, I will not be polemic: You are my truth.

If You strengthen me with grace, I will not hesitate: You are my life.

If You try me, I am not afraid of suffering: it is a sign of Your love.

If You want me to follow You, I will accept the cross: it leads to victory.

If You want me to be Your apostle, I am not afraid of my weakness: You are my strength.

Lord, in the calm and quiet moments of my life, be my joy.

In the sad and difficult moments, be my strength.

In the hour of darkness and defeat, be my light and happiness.

At the hour of my death, be my resurrection.

With You, Lord, I fear nothing; I am not alone. You have overcome death forever. Amen. Alleluia!

SECOND SUNDAY OF EASTER

The Sacrament of Penance

Readings: Acts 2:42-47
1 Peter 1:3-9
John 20:19-31

The first fruit of our Redemption is the forgiveness of sins. "Receive the Holy Spirit. If you forgive men's sins, they are forgiven them, if you hold them bound, they are held bound" (cf. Third Reading).

Through the history of the Church the Sacrament of Penance has had various formulations, applications and adaptations. This is quite natural, for the substance has never changed, but the Church has always adapted to the people and the times (cf. Const. on the Sacred Liturgy, no. 21). We all know that Vatican II has updated methods and introduced the new "Penitential Rite." The liturgical reform for the Sacrament of Penance includes three forms of reconciliation. The traditional individual form stresses, however, the importance of personal dispositions and the need of a personal relationship to the Word of God. The second form is a collective preparation followed by individual Confession and absolution; this form combines the communitarian and the individual acts. Group reconciliation and a single general absolution for all present is the third form. It is for particular occasions with approval of the bishop; however, if there are mortal sins they must be individually confessed later on.

What is more important for us are the effects of this Sacrament. It reunites offender and Offended; God is waiting for us, ready to embrace us as He did the prodigal son.

Through forgiveness of sins we regain direct communication with Christ, the eternal Word of God who never changes (cf. Hebrews 13:8). The Holy Spirit works through this Sacrament. The Holy Spirit enables us to understand our interior situation, giving us confidence and hope. Even when we have not broken our friendship with God, the Sacrament of Penance produces its effects. The Holy Spirit gives us the necessary energy to overcome our inclinations to sin.

Through this Sacrament the Christian grows in the three theological virtues: faith, hope and charity. To confess our sins is to have faith and to trust in the Word of God. We receive this Sacrament because we hope to regain or increase the life of God in us. In the Sacrament of Penance we give God a chance to show His love for us, and, since we have not been faithful to this love, we have the opportunity to seek pardon and absolution.

When we receive the Sacrament of Penance even the entire Church benefits from it. In Penance the individual is reunited to Christ, and the Church is purified and vitalized. Through this Sacrament, the Church renders our salvation visible.

Penance also has a social effect. To be with God or against Him is closely connected to being with or against our neighbors. The entire community benefits when we re-establish ourselves as adopted sons of God. Our position in society as Christians is very important. In the Sacrament of Penance we take responsibility for what we have failed to do for others, and we renew our intentions to build a better world. "Not only does the Sacrament of Penance repeat God's mercy and prepare us to meet God in the Eucharist, it is also a great burst of love which increases our social sensitivity..." (Paul VI, February 13, 1976).

PASTORAL REFLECTIONS

1. *The Sacrament of Penance is a means of sanctity.* "There can be no Redemption for mankind, no call to follow Christ or achieve spiritual perfection, without the frequent and intelligent use of this sacrament" (Paul VI, April 2, 1974). St. Charles Borromeo confessed his shortcomings every day to purify himself. St. John Bosco said that Dominic Savio reached great perfection because he knew how to use the Sacrament of Penance well. Penance is a new life; it is throwing one's self into God's love; it is being involved in the dynamics of salvation and sanctification. "Confession is a source of grace and peace, a school of Christianity, consolation in our journey towards eternal happiness" (Paul VI, May 2, 1976).

2. *The ministers of Penance should always be available* (cf. Decree on the Ministry and Life of Priests, no. 13). "Priests should cherish the art of caring for souls. It is not a question of giving your priesthood an individualistic character. It is a question of being faithful to your call to be ministers of God's grace, specialists in caring for souls" (Paul VI, April 3, 1974). "Brothers in the priesthood, be specialists in the ministry of salvation. It is a delicate and difficult task, but an excellent and immediate means of grace. It is therapy for souls, a

source of light and wisdom. It is an exercise in goodness. It is a school of humility for the minister. Take it seriously. Do not administer it in any old way and never profane it. The way you administer the Sacrament of Penance is an indication of your priestly charity" (Paul VI, March 12, 1975).

3. *What should be the attitude of the Christian towards Penance?* "We must remember, admire and rejoice over the fact that Christ has obtained this marvelous favor for us, the forgiveness of sins. Considering our commitment at Baptism, in a certain sense the need for forgiveness is illogical; it is an act of infinite goodness; it is our resurrection to the new life through the power of God" (Paul VI, February 26, 1975). "To trust in sacramental confession is difficult but consoling. It is an experience in divine mercy. To cure your body you carefully choose a doctor; for your souls you must also choose a wise minister of grace" (Paul VI, March 12, 1975).

THIRD SUNDAY OF EASTER

We Are Pilgrims

Readings: Acts 2:14, 22-28
1 Peter 1:17-21
Luke 24:13-35

The disciples making their way to Emmaus remind us that we too are pilgrims. The history of the chosen people is the history of pilgrims. Abram was called by God to go to a mysterious and holy place. Moses led God's people on their journey to the promised land. After they reached the promised land the Jewish people made a pilgrimage three times a year to Jerusalem. As a young boy, Jesus also went to Jerusalem.

After the resurrection and ascension, Palestine—and in particular Jerusalem—became the goal of Christian pilgrims. We know that St. Helen dedicated much time and effort to the holy places and to the assistance of those who visited them. Perhaps the earliest "diary" we have of a pilgrim is that of a Spanish lady by the name of Egeria (393-396 AD). She describes the conditions of the holy places and the movement of the pilgrims.

Emperor Constantine granted religious freedom in 313, and not long after, Rome and the burial places of Peter and Paul became the goal of many pilgrims. Later, when the holy places fell into the hands of the infidels (1291 AD), Christians could no longer visit the Holy Land, and Rome became the more popular goal of the pilgrims. Pope Boniface VIII organized the first Jubilee of the Church in 1300 precisely for the pilgrims. To make it possible for every generation to participate, Pope Sixtus V established that this Jubilee be celebrated every twenty-five years rather than every one-hundred years, and Pope Alexander VI prescribed that the Holy Year be opened on Christmas and closed the following Christmas.

On various occasions Pope Paul VI has given us the religious, social and pastoral significance of a pilgrimage. The following is a synthesis of his teaching.

1. More than anything else the purpose of a pilgrimage is to meet God. It cannot be an excuse for tourism. A pilgrim is one who leaves the ways of sin and goes to God. The best thing possible for man is to meet God; the most urgent need of creatures is to be reconciled with God (cf. Paul VI, June 20, 1973).

2. A pilgrimage is a material and psychological separation. The pilgrim leaves his home, his possessions, to go elsewhere. In contact with new people and new places, at times we are invited to leave behind our ideas and we become "poor in spirit" in view of an interior renewal. A pilgrimage presupposes interior freedom (cf. Paul VI, May 9, 1973 and November 11, 1973).

3. A pilgrimage has a communitarian value. It is an occasion to examine our ability to communicate with others, to correct our social defects. It is a commitment to show that we do love our neighbors (cf. Paul VI, May 16, 1973).

4. The difficulties of a pilgrimage have an ascetic value. On any trip there are problems, unforeseen difficulties, and the bother of having to live with others. Through these sufferings we can participate in the sufferings of Christ and strengthen our friendship with Him. In the early Church the sinner had to do public penance; in a certain sense this is what the pilgrim does (cf. Paul VI, November 10, 1973).

5. Having left many things behind, the pilgrim can more easily find time and silence for prayer and meditation. He will have time to get to know the more famous pilgrims starting with Abram to St. Paul, from the Virgin Mary to those who have dedicated their lives to the apostolate (cf. Paul VI, December 5, 1973).

6. The early Christians came to Rome to visit the tombs of Peter and Paul and to receive advice and encouragement to live their lives of faith; the motivation is still the same. "The pilgrim Church comes from every country of the world to gather in the unforgettable square in front of St. Peter's Basilica, the meeting place for those who accept Christ" (Paul VI, December 29, 1973).

7. There is an eschatological value in a pilgrimage: pilgrims are people going towards eternity, towards the city of the future (cf. Hebrews 13:14), a city with its doors open (cf. Revelation 21:23-25), in which Christ is the source of light and eternal life (cf. Paul VI, November 29, 1973).

8. A pilgrimage also has an apostolic value. The holy places are visited to obtain the energy necessary to live the Christian life with more commitment and authenticity "in a modified and correct relation with the world and with our fellow men" (Paul VI, November 21, 1973).

9. A pilgrimage is an historical occasion during which our Christian life can develop. There can be a new outlook, a new intention to live our evangelical life more generously (cf. Paul VI, January 22 and 26, 1976).

10. The final and lasting goal of a pilgrimage is peace. When man lives the ascetic spiritual values of the Christian life, he will contribute to the real peace in the world (cf. Paul VI, January 1, 1975).

PASTORAL REFLECTIONS

1. *The renewal must be within man.* A pilgrimage offers the possibility of an interior renewal. In the Old Testament the journey was to meet someone: to meet God. In the New Testament, where God is with us, the purpose of the journey is a spiritual change. Using the force and energy coming from Christ, it is always possible to improve our relations with God, with men, with the Church and with the world. "Man must return to his original state of goodness" (Paul VI, January 1, 1975).

2. *Mary should be our traveling companion.* Mary, the mother of Jesus and the mother of the Church, knows the way to Christ. She will also protect us from the dangers along the way.

3. *A Prayer.*
I have come to You, Lord, as a pilgrim to recall that my life is a pilgrimage, a journey towards heaven. I was loaded with worry and fatigue, I had hoped to unload it all and finally live free. But I misunderstood Your words, Lord. Your gift of love is also a commitment, a duty, a sacrifice. I have now entered the temple of faith and love. I have found a new dimension. I have found my fellowmen. I am beginning to understand love. I am beginning to experience joy.

FOURTH SUNDAY OF EASTER

Authority in the Church

> Readings: Acts 2:14, 36-41
> 1 Peter 2:20-25
> John 10:1-10

If we undertake a journey to an unknown place we need someone to show us the way. The Third Reading of today's Liturgy offers excellent material to meditate on the difficult combination: authority-obedience.

There is much tension today between leader and collaborator, between ecclesiastical authority and the faithful. Certainly one of the reasons for this is man's instinctive aversion for authority. It is no secret that through the centuries there have been representatives of authority in the Church who were authoritarian. Perhaps the reaction is not in proportion to the facts. One of the more widespread ideas today is that ecclesiastical authority is nothing more and nothing less than civil authority. It is true that, at times, "what is Caesar's" and "what is God's" coincide in their external juridical manifestations, but they are not the same. Civil authority does not generate life and much less supernatural life. The bishop, through his full participation in the humanity of Christ, is father and teacher, and through the bishop the community becomes the Church and the life-giving mother.

At times science and its research tend to undermine our concept of authority. The goal of any science is to progress in the knowledge of its proper object through research and hypothesis. The object of faith is the unchangeable concepts which have been given to us and are summarized in the Creed. There can be progress in our knowledge and application of these concepts, but the facts of faith are always the same. It is the bishop's duty to safeguard this deposit of faith. His authority stems from this obligation to protect the truth. Hasty conclusions about decentralization and pluralism can also interfere in the relations between bishops and priests, between hierarchy and theologians, between pastors and faithful. In the past, the diocese, the parish and the religious congregations were ruled absolutely by the bishop, the pastor and the superior.

As the Christian matures in his community, he is invited to be more responsible. Thus we have the various diocesan and parish councils and commissions. Enlarging the field of responsibility means increasing the possibility of conflict between faithful and pastors, between pastors and bishops, between bishops and the Holy Father. In any passage from the theoretical to the practical there are difficulties. The local church is authentic when it accepts its priests together with the Gospels and the Eucharist, and the priests accept the bishop (cf. Dogmatic Const. on the Church, no. 26). The bishop's position of authority is one of the original truths of the Church. Jesus chose some with the intention that they lead the rest (cf. Matthew 18:18; Acts 20:28). Already in the second century St. Ignatius of Antioch wrote: "Without the bishops there is no Church." In the third century St. Cyprian wrote: "The bishop is in the Church and the Church is in the bishop." The various Councils through the centuries have always stressed the duty of the bishops: "to feed the people of God." Vatican II leaves no room for doubt about the position of the bishops in the Church (cf. Decree on the Ministry and Life of Priests, nos. 7 and 8).

It is not exact to say that the primitive Church was founded on individual charisms. They were highly respected, but we all know that Paul and Barnabas went to Jerusalem, to Peter, to settle the difference of opinion about the qualifications for Christianity (cf. Acts 15:1-4).

PASTORAL REFLECTIONS

1. *Through the Spirit of God union can become communion.* There will always be differences of opinion

and evaluation. To achieve unity within our mental and dynamic differences we need the Holy Spirit. The human body has many different organs and members, but there is only one vital principle giving them life. In the Church there can be, and there are, various manifestations. The individual can have his particular function, provided all have the same vital principle. There is unity and communion in the Mystical Body of Christ, because it is vitalized by the Holy Spirit.

2. *Authority presupposes certain obligations.* The episcopate is not simply a dignity or an honor. It is a function, a ministry and a service. The bishop is a pastor. The good shepherd gives his life for his sheep, as Jesus did. The good shepherd lives for his sheep. If one intends to be a leader of the People of God, he must give himself totally to love them and to serve them (cf. Paul VI, June 30, 1974, and February 10, 1975).

3. *The faithful together with their priests must respond to the love of their bishop.* The characteristics of the response are availability, trust, sincerity, friendship, obedience to the voice of the Spirit, ability to participate in and carry out the operative indications even if they are not completely to our way of thinking. St. Ignatius of Antioch wrote to his Christians: "Your priests should be united to the bishop as the cords of a lyre so that Christ may be praised by the unity of Sacraments and the symphony of love...." Pope Paul repeats the same concept. "In forming the new ecclesial mentality we must develop a sense of communion. We must be aware of our liberty and personality and at the same time we must remember that we are neither alone nor autonomous. We must feel and live our independence and responsibility and this presupposes participation in a community and hierarchy. The two attitudes are developed together in mutual respect. This is what it means to be a Catholic: united and universal..." (Paul VI, November 12, 1968, and January 8, 1975).

FIFTH SUNDAY OF EASTER

The Priesthood of the Faithful

Readings: Acts 6:1-7
1 Peter 2:4-9
John 14:1-12

In the early era of Christianity the priesthood of the faithful was vivid and active (cf. Second Reading). Because of various historical events through the centuries it was more or less forgotten. Vatican II has reinserted the laity in its effective role as a "royal priesthood" of the People of God. This has improved the Church's vertical dimension, the relations between the hierarchy and the faithful. Horizontally this has inserted the Church in the vicissitudes of the modern world. In their "priesthood," the faithful are a spiritual reality within the earthly reality. There is no foundation whatsoever for that old erroneous idea that evil is in the world and good is in the Church. There is no reason to separate the Christian united in faith with the hierarchy from the rest of men absorbed in their work and immersed in the historical and social events of mankind. The antithesis between the heavenly City and the earthly city, popular in the Constantinian era, does not exist. The Christian, the Catholic layman, can and must animate the world.

This is also necessary because there is a shortage of priests. The Church needs the laity to realize her sociocultural contribution to the world. Like the small amount of yeast in the flour, some Christians must be mixed in the masses of humanity if they are to be enriched and saved.

The individual layman who accepts to live his "priesthood" in the world will benefit personally; he will experience satisfaction. Deep within our person there is a desire to unite and integrate all things. This, however, is not easy. Is an hour or so a week of direct contact with

God in the Church or parish sufficient to obtain the necessary supernatural strength to live in and animate even a small portion of the world so full of problems? Besides the problems of the world there are personal difficulties, a family to look after, and similar concerns; and the temptation to "do things in any old way just to get them done" can be very great.

It is a delicate mission and a great responsibility; it means being both man and Christian, layman and theologian, technician and "priest."

Every creature is a world to himself with a tendency to constant change depending on the psychological moments. This obviously makes it difficult for the apostle to get in contact with his fellow man; he will have to update his methods frequently (cf. Decree on the Ministry and Life of Priests, no. 19). To work with the simple and invisible reality of souls is not the same as to work with material objects. These difficulties are not mentioned to discourage or frighten the laity but to stimulate and encourage them.

PASTORAL REFLECTIONS

The Catholic layman can influence the world in many ways, following the indications of St. Peter (cf. Second Reading). Here are three points:

1. *We must know and be enthusiastic about the word of God.* Social reality changes rapidly, and yet it must be possible to apply our faith to any and every situation. To achieve an anthropological integration of faith, the apostle must thoroughly know the word of God, he must know how to apply the word of God and thus sanctify the actual situation. A theology for the laity is necessary today if they are to continue to be the chosen People of God (cf. Pastoral Const. on the Church in the Modern World, no. 62).

2. *The apostle cannot be totally immersed in the world.* He is a member of a "holy people." Philosophical-

ly the apostle is the "logos" of all that is human, in practice he is the "logos" of action, and theologically he is the "logos" of the divine. The divine must animate the world. If the divine is confused with the world, how can it be animated? "If salt has lost its taste, how shall its saltness be restored?" (Matthew 5:13) To live for others means essentially to bring them something they are lacking. Uniformity is unproductive; diversity can be that mystical component which changes and elevates history (cf. Paul VI, November 21, 1973).

3. *The pastoral strategy* of the apostle will be easier and more fruitful if it is centered on the person of Christ. The goal of the "royal priesthood" is to bring others to Christ by sharing with them our interior enthusiasm. In this way there can be even right social change. We must not, however, be worried about numbers. Moses was alone; so was Elias, Paul, and others. Christ after His resurrection appeared to only a few chosen witnesses (cf. Acts 2:32). The source of life is one and the application of salvation is effected by a few.

SIXTH SUNDAY OF EASTER

The Sacrament of Confirmation

Readings: Acts 8:5-8, 14-17
1 Peter 3:15-18
John 14:15-21

If there should be doubts about the spiritual priesthood of the faithful, some reflections on the Sacrament of Confirmation will help to strengthen this concept.

This sacrament is both a gift of the Holy Spirit and a commission to the apostolate. The entire Christian life is a gift of the Holy Spirit. In Baptism the Holy Spirit makes us new creatures. In Confirmation we reach maturity and are ready for action as members of Christ. In a certain sense Confirmation is the perfection and completion of Baptism. Maturity and perfection presuppose external relations. The need for the apostolate is a necessary consequence of Confirmation, and this is clear from the charismatic richness of this sacrament. There is an evident comparison between the confirmed Christian and Jesus; who after His Baptism in the Jordan received the Holy Spirit and began His apostolate. Throughout the history and teaching of the Church this anointing has always been considered as a special grace and an invitation to begin apostolic action. Confirmation completes the internal transformation and qualification and supplies the necessary strength and courage to witness Christ. The liturgy of this sacrament clearly indicates the new position of the Christian in relation to the kingdom of Christ.

The confirmed Christian has a right to participate in the life and action of the Church. Consequently, the local Church should make every effort to receive this new apostle. It is the task of the People of God to prepare the candidates for Confirmation. Usually this is nothing more than a series of instructions. It is important that the candidate for Confirmation be introduced to the word of God, participate actively in the liturgy and begin a certain operative commitment. The entire ecclesial community should participate in the celebration of this sacrament. It should be a day of festivity when the presence of the Holy Spirit becomes visible in the Christian community.

The candidate for Confirmation must be well prepared. This involves various members of the Christian community. The bishop must see to it that the candidate has a comprehensive knowledge of his Christian commitment. The parents should help to introduce the candidate to the sacramental life of a Christian; the most effective way is through example. The godparents, if possible the same as in Baptism, should be worthy to present the candidate to the Church. In other words, they too must belong to the Church and live their faith in such a way as to be co-responsible for the spiritual and apostolic growth of the candidate.

The candidate for Confirmation must be aware that through this gift of the Holy Spirit he will be marked forever as belonging to Christ and to the Church. He must prepare himself seriously. Through this sacrament he will be totally and operatively involved in God's infinite love.

PASTORAL REFLECTIONS

1. *The confirmed Christian is one who opposes evil.* St. Paul puts it a little differently when he encourages the Ephesians to hold up their shield against sin (cf. Ephesians 6:16). Confirmation renders our faith active and makes us capable of overcoming evil.

2. *The main task of the confirmed Christian is to communicate the Good News, to transmit God's message.* The mission of the Christian is to preach Christ everywhere. He is the messenger of truth. There is a great gap between the word of God and the world; the masses no longer receive the authentic message of religion.

3. Above all, the confirmed Christian is a generous person. *His vocation is to love all men.* Through his positive way of life the Christian disintoxicates society and gives life to the Church. The Christian is distinguished by his love for and identification with his fellow men. He prefers the folly of charity to the shrewdness of egoism.

ASCENSION THURSDAY

The Ascension of Jesus

Readings: Acts 1:1-11
Ephesians 1:17-23
Matthew 28:16-20

St. Luke records this historical event in all its details (cf. First Reading). He gives a particular significance to the Ascension. In a certain sense it is more important for him than the crucifixion and resurrection. By His Incarnation Christ has come in the flesh, and He will come again in glory. These are two fundamental points of reference for Luke. Considering the history of our salvation in this way, the Ascension becomes the connection between these two facts. By His birth Christ overcomes the infinite distance between God and man; by His Ascension He unites man to his Creator. The Bible frequently speaks of the heavens as God's country and the earth as man's territory. Christ united these two extremities. Remaining God, He became man. By His Ascension Christ has re-established permanent communication between time and eternity, between the finite and the Infinite. Jacob visualized this communication in a dream as a ladder from earth to heaven. During His short stay with us on earth Christ brought us a new way of life, but the best news is the fact that He will return "just as you saw Him go up into the heavens" (cf. First Reading). This fact is so important for Luke that he records it twice, at the end of his Gospel and at the beginning of the Acts. The entire life of Jesus was directed towards the Ascension; in the same manner, the Christian way of life is directed towards the transfiguration of humanity. The "Parousia"—the second glorious coming of Christ—will end the pilgrimage of humanity.

The Ascension has introduced for man a new era, which has various characteristic interior components. The Gospels call our attention to the transcendence of

God: "...then he was lifted up before their eyes in a cloud which took him from their sight" (cf. First Reading). In the Old Testament the cloud was the vehicle of God's presence (cf. Numbers 11:25). The cloud—the transcendence of God—is also part of the transfiguration on Mt. Tabor. God is near man, visible in His humanity, but in His essence He is completely above man's intellectual capacities. He is beyond any descriptive classification. By nature God is infinite, transcendent. "God, You are beyond all that exists, You are unknowable even if all our thoughts come from You. You are all things, and yet it is impossible for me to give You a name because You alone cannot be contained in a name" (St. Gregory of Nazianzen). The social dimension of our salvation embraces the mysterious essence of God. After the Ascension, God is physically absent yet present in the Church, in the Sacraments, in the hierarchy, in our neighbors, in everyone. He is hidden and active even in the most ordinary events of our life, in our common everyday contacts with others.

This new relationship between Christ and the faithful, after the Ascension, is based on faith. "The Ascension of the Lord was very beneficial for the Apostles. It was only after the Ascension that they began to orient their contemplation towards the divinity of Christ, seeing that His body was, perhaps, an obstacle to the mystery of His divinity. The second Person of the Trinity was never separated from the Father during His stay on earth, nor is He separated from His followers after His return to the Father. The mysterious presence of His divinity increased when His human presence disappeared. Beginning with the Ascension, faith opens the way to the Son of God" (Pope Leo the Great, Homily II for the Ascension).

Hope is another aspect of the new era after the Ascension. Man's history is no longer just an earthly linear succession of events. It now has a vertical dimension: man is directed towards God. Christ has ascended high above the heavens, that He might fill all of us with

His gifts (cf. Ephesians 4:10), and through the Holy Spirit reveal the truth to men (cf. John 16:7). This is true even today when it seems that doubt has contaminated society and handicapped the Church. God, Creator of the world, is not playing games with the world. His promise follows a slow and mysterious plan, but it will triumph even if at times it seems to be involved in the vicissitudes of light and darkness, of success and failure, of life and death.

Apostolic and missionary charity is another component of the feast of the Ascension. The disciples who witnessed all the marvels of Christ's life were invited to return to Jerusalem and from there to bring the good news of Redemption and love to all nations. The primitive Christian communities were outstanding in their pastoral activity. Their longing for the future and their certainty that Christ will return gave them courage and apostolic vigor. They were able to transform everything into what they loved and what they had seen.

PASTORAL REFLECTIONS

1. *Our longing for God* is not something added or imposed; it *is a fundamental requisite of our being.* Life, whether it be individual or in a group, always tends to better itself. Man is never really satisfied with what he has or what he is. He is forever seeking something just a little bit better. This constant illusion, which comes from contact with the finite reality of earth, directs us to God; He alone can satisfy our most intimate desires.

2. Wanting to better earthly reality can be quite trivial; *the alternative is to be aware of our final goal.* The simplest way to free ourselves of egoism is to live our supernatural vocation coherently. To be authentically man and Christian, it is necessary to project ourselves towards the infinite. By His Ascension Christ opens the way to eternity, and through the centuries man has gone and still does go this way. The Ascension reminds us that we are candidates for eternity.

3. *What do we have to do?* We can prepare ourselves and in a certain sense begin to enjoy our eternal encounter with God. Acceptance of the Word of God and prayer are essential to our life with God. Through our acceptance of the Word, God comes to us, and through prayer we return to Him.

SEVENTH SUNDAY OF EASTER

Prayer and the Church

Readings: Acts 1:12-14
1 Peter 4:13-16
John 17:1-11

Prayer is the strength of every Christian, the classical tool of every apostolate, the soul of every ecclesial meeting. St. Luke gives us an excellent image of the primitive Church: "All these with one accord devoted themselves to prayer, together with the women and Mary the Mother of Jesus, and with his brothers" (First Reading).

Man normally has knowledge of nature, of himself, of others and of God. To complete this fourfold dimension man needs to communicate. Man's need for prayer is also seen in the intuition of the divine Presence. "Accepting the existence of God, it is spontaneous that man wants to communicate with Him. Prayer is the first dialogue that man wants with God. If God exists and I can reach Him, then I must communicate with Him. Prayer is a spiritual and moral necessity for man, a normal and habitual attitude of a creature in relation to his Creator" (Paul VI, January 30, 1974).

Prayer is the breath of the soul, the life of a Christian. The Christian not only knows God, but also communicates with Him. Seen in this perspective the language of the adopted son of God becomes, necessarily, prayer. Above all, prayer is the voice of the

Church. The first Christian community distinguished itself by praying together. This common prayer is the sign and cause of the community: sign, inasmuch as it qualifies the community as the Church of Christ; cause, inasmuch as it is the reason for the unity. Those who participate in common prayer are united in love as the Trinity (cf. Decree on the Ministry and Life of Priests, no. 8). In community prayer, isolation and individualism are overcome; romantic devotion is eliminated. The community becomes the voice of Christ. In common prayer human solitude disappears. There is a communication between members of the same family: the Church; between children of the same Father: God. The most intimate Church is man's heart.

Perhaps the best and simplest methodology of prayer is the invocation the Apostles used: "Lord, teach us to pray" (cf. Luke 11:1).

It is through faith, hope and charity that prayer becomes the language of the adopted children of God. Consequently, these virtues should be evident in our prayer. Without faith it is impossible to hear and accept the Word of God. We can respond only after we have heard the Word of God (cf. Luke 11:27; John 7:6).

Christian prayer is nourished by hope. The thought that God listens to us, is good to us and wants to help us is a certitude for the Christian. We must not let our earthly and commercial way of thinking enter our prayer, that is, pretend that prayer is the easy remedy for every temporal need.

Every act of prayer is an act of adoration and friendship with God. At times our prayers will seem to be useless. God's love for us is infinite. He has a plan for us. Trust in prayer should not be shaken because we do not get what we have asked for. The monks of the Himalayas pray: "Lord, we do not know what is good for us; you do. For this reason we pray to you and thank you." Prayer is never useless, at the proper moment our heavenly Father will reply.

Prayer is charity. In prayer we praise, glorify and thank the Lord for His infinite goodness towards us, for Redeeming us and His mercy for us. "If we were diligent in thanking God for all He has given us, we would have no time to complain" (James Alberione, Founder of the Pauline Family). Authentic prayer seeks God's love and mercy. The prayer of the primitive Church is synthesized in the expression: "Lord, have mercy on us." Love should dominate our conversations with our God. Prayer is being together with our Father, communicating with Him, listening to Him, enjoying His presence, that is, loving Him. A heart without words is better than many words without a heart.

PASTORAL REFLECTIONS

1. *Activity cannot be separated from prayer.* Saint Charles Borromeo once said to one of his priests: "Do not give yourself totally to activity for others so as not to have time for yourself, time for prayer...." Alexis Carrel points out that the elimination of prayer foretells the fall of a civilization or a religion. If the engine of an airplane fails, the airplane falls; if a Christian fails to pray, moral disaster is near. Statistical research has revealed that most spiritual crises for Christians, religious and priests began with the loss of interest in prayer. The human personality rests on three basic needs: solidarity, liberty and an interior life. In prayer they are expressed and fulfilled. The philosopher Henri Bergson said: "Through prayer we can free ourselves of the material and hedonistic civilization and live according to our lofty desires as immortal creatures."

2. *Prayer is the life of the Church.* "The life and breath of the Church is prayer. When two or more are gathered together in His name He is with them (cf. Matthew 18:26). The Spirit inflames our hearts and intercedes for us because we are weak, we do not know what to pray for, nor how to ask for it (cf. Romans 8:26). The triumphant, the militant and the suffering members

of the Church are all united by the common bond of prayer. Prayer is the instruction of the saints, the vocation of the priests. Peter and the Apostles knew the importance of concentrating on prayer and the ministry of the word (cf. Acts 6:4). Prayer is company for the family, strength for the innocent, grace for youth, hope for old age and comfort for the dying" (Paul VI, April 27, 1969).

3. *Prayer is the life and mission of those who have consecrated themselves to God.* (cf. Decree on the Appropriate Renewal of the Religious Life, nos. 7; 15). Saint Teresa of Avila wanted the convent to be the representation of man before God. The renewal of Carmel was a return to prayer. St. Thérèse of the Child Jesus considered prayer as her main task: "I came to the convent to save souls and to pray for priests." St. Anthony of Padua often said: "When you wake up in the morning, praise the Lord in the name of all mankind."

PENTECOST SUNDAY

The Holy Spirit and Renewal

Readings: Acts 2:1-11
1 Corinthians 12:3-7, 12-13
John 20:19-23

There is a certain continuity and interdependence of Christian Pentecost on the Jewish Pentecost. The Jewish Pentecost established a covenant of friendship with God that was juridical, exterior, restrictive, and temporary, in preparation for a new and more profound interior relationship between God and man. The Christian Pentecost is this new convenant with all humanity. Pentecost is the birth of God's people, that is, the universal Church with its universal mission. The bonds between God and His people are no longer juridical or exterior. They are interior and depend on personal responsibility. The benefits are not temporal but spiritual and supernatural.

"When the Son had completed His task on earth, the Father sent the Holy Spirit to sanctify the Church, thus making it possible for the faithful to be united to the Father in the same Spirit. That same Spirit gives life, dwells in the Church and in the hearts of man and witnesses to the fact that they are adopted sons of God. This Spirit gives the Church the whole truth and unites and directs the Church through the various hierarchical and charismatic gifts. He embellishes the Church with His gifts and constantly renews the Church with the strength of the Gospels. Overwhelmed by this Spirit, our life and events take on a new meaning. They have a truth which is above anything human" (Paul VI, Oct. 16, 1974).

It is easy to imagine that the Holy Spirit takes delight in the individual members of the Church. Christian life means life with this Spirit. In the spiritual sense the faithful becomes the object of divine love, and in the operative sense he uses the gifts, also called "charisms," for the benefit of others and in particular for the community. It is through these gifts that the Christian appreciates the life of Jesus, accepts His resurrection, enjoys His promises, and awaits His return. The effects of the Holy Spirit in the hearts of men are endless. Some of them are hidden trust, disinterested goodness, silent obedience, firm conviction that God's mercy is greater than our sins, generous love of prayer, patience in suffering, joy and happiness of spirit (cf. Galatians 5:22).

If we are to have a civilization of God's people, we must let ourselves be invaded and saturated by the Holy Spirit. Man can choose to remain simply man and refuse to be an adopted son of God. If the Holy Spirit is excluded, virtue is false, all knowledge is partial, and every action is insufficient. St. Augustine once said: "The only civilization is that of the Spirit." Only this civilization can act universally without being limited by man. As

Christians it is our duty and privilege to entrust ourselves to the Holy Spirit in order to form the community which can sanctify man's history (cf. Paul VI, June 6, 1972).

PASTORAL REFLECTIONS

1. *The Holy Spirit must be a part of the life of every Christian.* Without the Holy Spirit, God is far away, Christ is simply a historical person, the Gospels are early literary works, the Church is just another organization, authority is power, missionary activity is propaganda, liturgy is clinging to things of the past, and human activity is slavery. With the Holy Spirit, the entire cosmos is God's kingdom, Christ is risen and present, the Gospels are a vital force, the Church is communication with the Trinity, authority becomes service, the liturgy is an anticipation of the mystical, and human activity has an eternal value. The Holy Spirit is the love of God in us, the principle of truth, the font of all charisms, the inspiration of our thoughts, the strength of our actions, the voice of our prayers, our hope, our joy!

2. *The Holy Spirit is the soul of the Church.* If we are outside, or, worse yet, against the Church, how can we expect to be animated and enlightened by the Holy Spirit? St. Augustine said the same thing in a very clear and practical way: "The Holy Spirit acts in the Church as the soul does in the body. If part of the body is amputated, for example a finger or a foot, does the soul continue to animate the severed member? When part of the body, that member had life, but separated from the body it loses its life. It is the same for the Christian: separated from the body that is animated by the Holy Spirit, he loses this Spirit."

3. This meditation concludes with the Pentecost hymn written by Cardinal Stephan Langton, Archbishop of Canterbury, at the beginning of the thirteenth century. It is such a complete synthesis of our invocations to

the Holy Spirit that it has become part of the liturgy. "Come, Holy Spirit, come! And from thy celestial home shed a ray of light divine! Come, Father of the poor! Come, source of all our store! Come, within our bosoms shine! Thou, of comforters the best; thou, the soul's most welcome guest; sweet refreshment here below; in our labor, rest most sweet; grateful coolness in the heat; solace in the midst of woe. O most blessed Light divine, shine within these hearts of thine, and our inmost being fill! Where thou art not, man has naught, nothing good in deed or thought, nothing free from taint of ill. Heal our wounds, our strength renew; on our dryness pour thy dew; wash the stains of guilt away: bend the stubborn heart and will; melt the frozen, warm the chill; guide the steps that go astray. On the faithful, who adore and confess thee, evermore, in thy sev'nfold gifts descend; give them virtue's sure reward; give them thy salvation, Lord; give them joys that never end."

TRINITY SUNDAY

The Trinity in Our History and Our Lives

Readings: Exodus 34:4-6, 8-9
2 Corinthians 13:11-13
John 3:16-18

The mystery of the Trinity comes forth in all its glory in the New Testament. The authors of the New Testament give us a marvelous mosaic of the one divine nature and the three divine Persons. The Church has always defended this doctrine with exceptional vigor. Already in the year 325, during the Council of Nicea, the Church proclaimed the plurality of Persons and the unity of nature using a very human language intended for the people of that time. This Council formally refused the theory of Arius who denied the divinity of Christ.

The Councils of Ephesus (431) and Chalcedon (541) reconfirmed this truth giving particular attention to the Person and divinity of the Holy Spirit. This wonderful mystery has been part of every Council; it is superfluous to list them here. We know that the pastoral richness of Vatican II is based on the dynamic principle of the Holy Trinity. In the Decree on the Missionary Activity of the Church we read: "This decree flows from 'that fountain of love' or charity within God the Father. From Him, who is the 'origin without origin,' the Son is begotten and the Holy Spirit proceeds through the Son. Freely creating us out of His surpassing and merciful kindness, and graciously calling us, moreover, to communicate in life and glory with Himself, He has generously poured out His divine goodness and does not cease to do so" (Decree on the Missionary Activity of the Church, no. 2).

The Fathers of the Church consider this truth as the source of sanctification and the apostolate. St. Clement, at the end of the first century, wrote: "We have one God, one Christ and one Holy Spirit whose grace we have all received." St. Ignatius of Antioch wrote to his Christians: "Be strong in the faith and in charity with the Son, with the Father and with the Holy Spirit." St. Justin, in reply to the accusation that Christians were atheists, said: "We adore the Creator of the universe, the Son and the Holy Spirit." We could go on for the rest of the day recalling outstanding quotations about the Trinity. The message is very clear: Christianity is based on the solemn truth that there is one God in three divine Persons.

Human reason cannot comprehend the mystery of the Trinity. If man could grasp this truth, then God would be a finite reality which can be contained in human intelligence. There are many similarities in nature which help man to accept this truth. St. Augustine was an expert in finding these comparisons: "We have a memory, an intellect and a will and yet we are one person. Our personality has a threefold expression: evaluation, sentiment, and an artistic sense. There is a trinity of time: the past, the present, and the future. In our lives there are youth, maturity and old age. Our sense knowledge is a single act, yet it involves the object, the image and the idea and all three come from the same object. This similarity is most clear in our souls: the soul is the single mysterious principle of our lives and yet it is the source of our faith, our hope, and our charity."

Today's feast is much more than a dogma to conserve, a theological truth which is a sort of test for our intellectual ability. The Trinity is the best expression we have of God's fullness and perfection. The life of God is so infinitely full it cannot be contained in the knowledge, love and action of a single "Ego"; as it were, three "Egos" are needed, that is, three ways of being in which knowledge, will and love are elevated to the fullness of a personal existence. God is really and personally Father, Son and Holy Spirit. This entire threefold divine life is the essence of our supernatural vocation. Dionysius of Alexandria used a comparison from nature to help grasp this aspect of the Trinity. The external manifestation of a spring is water which becomes a stream. The source of life is the Father who, in the Son, becomes the water of salvation and this water of grace penetrates the streams of the Holy Spirit giving life to souls; then this water returns to its source by the power of the Holy Spirit. Saint Paul ends his second letter to the Corinthians with a beautiful hymn to the Trinity: "The grace of the Lord Jesus Christ, and the love of God, and the fellowship of the Holy Spirit be with you all" (Second Reading).

PASTORAL REFLECTIONS

1. *Every Christian is called to praise and thank the Holy Trinity.* Nothing, not even death, could turn the early Christians from this duty. St. Polycarp sang the praises of the Holy Trinity as his executioners lighted the fire in which he died. When St. Apollinaris was condemned to death by a Roman proconsul, he said: "I thank my God together with all those who know His

Son, Jesus Christ, and the Holy Spirit for this condemnation which is my salvation." We are not called to such heroism, but it should be possible for us to respect the name of God. The Sign of the Cross is a symbol and a prayer to the Trinity; this simple sign reveals our faith in the Trinity.

2. *United to the Trinity we will grow in our spiritual life.* The liturgy has us recite the "Credo" during every festive Mass. This beautiful declaration invites us to accept the history of our salvation and to grow in that marvelous communion with the Father, the Son and the Holy Spirit. The mature Christian lives his fellowship with the Trinity.

3. *A Prayer.* Trinity of love, plurality of Persons yet perfect unity, make our community resemble your unity. Give us your love so we can overcome our differences, and our urge for competition. Give us the energy of your charity so that we can accept the sacrifices necessary to get along with others. Fill our hearts with joy when living with and working for others becomes burdensome. Join our souls together in a living community of love which is united to you, most Holy Trinity.

THE FEAST OF *CORPUS CHRISTI*

The Bread of Angels

Readings: Deuteronomy 8:2-3, 14-16
1 Corinthians 10:16-17
John 6:51-58

There are various reasons why the Church celebrates the solemnity of the Eucharist.

The Eucharist is the life of the Church. Every aspect of cult, every liturgical expression has the Eucharist as its goal and its completion. The other sacraments are a preparation for the Eucharist. It is only in the Eucharist that perfect union with Christ is possible. The Church really exists where there is a Eucharistic mentality and where there are enthusiastic witnesses to the "Bread of Life." The two disciples recognized their traveling companion when He broke bread with them. If the Church did not have the specific mission to break bread with her members it would be easy to think of the Church as just another organization, a human society, based on historic reality.

The Holy Eucharist qualifies the priestly vocation. "The ministry of the priesthood embraces, penetrates and becomes one with the ministry of the Eucharist. Who, more than the priest, can say in a mystical and authentic reality: 'It is no longer I who live, but Christ lives in me.' Christ calls each one of us His friend; He has given us (priests) the wonderful power to consecrate the Eucharist. Could He have given a greater proof of His trust in us? Our personal choice to serve the Church in the ministry of the Eucharist should not be questioned. My fellow priests and all Christians, we must thank the Lord for the Eucharist. Our glory, our strength and our comfort is in the Eucharist" (Paul VI, March 27, 1975).

The Eucharist is the joy of our lives. Throughout the entire history of man there has been, and still is, a tendency of God to meet man and a tendency of man to meet God. The meeting has taken place. The Incarnation is the historical fact; and the Eucharist is the vital, universal continuation of this meeting. Man's dream to possess God is realized in the Eucharist. Christ was present in Palestine and spent His time doing good to His fellow men. In our churches Christ is present under the appearance of bread and wine. He is always available to listen to our problems, to enlighten and console us. On Calvary Christ sacrificed Himself for our Redemption; through the Eucharist this sacrifice is renewed.

Our salvation is a series of marvels of love. First marvel: God becomes man (the Incarnation); second marvel: the Incarnate God becomes our food (the Eucharist); third marvel: the immolated Lamb becomes our eternal beatitude (heaven). God became flesh (Christmas) to remain with us in the Church (Eucharist), to show us His glory (heaven). The bond between the Eucharist and Paradise is clearly illustrated in the liturgy of the Mass when we say: "When we eat this bread and drink this cup, we proclaim your death, Lord Jesus, until you come in glory." St. Thomas describes the Eucharist as "angelic Bread, Food of the pilgrims on their way to their divine fatherland."

The Eucharist is the center of the universe. Scientifically the sun is the center of our planetary system, but the earth is the historic center of the universe. God became man on earth; the Eucharist "God dwelling among men" (cf. Revelation 21:3) is present on earth. In appearance the Eucharist is a small piece of bread; in reality It is the magnificence and power of God. It is the life and support of Christians throughout the world.

PASTORAL REFLECTIONS

1. *The Eucharist is the real presence of Christ.* This presence in the Eucharist is a mystery of love. Christ said: "I will not leave you orphans, I will come to you." After His resurrection this promise became a reality. God is with us, Christ is with us: "I am with you always, until the end of the ages" (Matthew 28:20). Wherever the Eucharist is celebrated, there the mystery of Christ's Real Presence is revealed and proclaimed.

2. *The presence of Christ in the Eucharist is a sign of His individual love for us.* One of the mysterious aspects of the Eucharist is the divine Presence in the numberless churches throughout the world. One voice can be heard by all the people who listen to it; one word can give rise to as many thoughts as there are people who understand it. One Christ is present wherever the sacramental signs are: to be totally available for each one of us.

3. *His Presence in the Eucharist is an invitation.* "Come to me, all who labor and are heavy laden, and I will give you rest" (Matthew 11:28). Christ's invitation is the invitation of a friend who patiently waits, ready to receive everyone. If there is any preference, it is for

those who are lost and lonely, for those who are confused, for those who suffer the emptiness of material things. "Come, I am the Way, the Truth and the Life" (cf. John 14:6).

SECOND SUNDAY IN ORDINARY TIME

Sanctity is the Goal of Religion

Readings: Isaiah 49:3, 5-6
1 Corinthians 1:1-3
John 1:29-34

Sanctity is the duty of every Christian; it should not be an exceptional characteristic of a few, or much less, a hobby for those who like to be different. Christ has frequently invited us to be "holy because He is holy," to be "perfect as the heavenly Father is perfect." St. Paul said that it is the will of God that we be saints, for we have been created, chosen and redeemed in view of our sanctification. Vatican II speaks quite clearly: "In the Church, every one belonging to the hierarchy, or being cared for by it, is called to holiness" (Dogmatic Constitution on the Church, no. 39). "The followers of Christ...by God's gifts must hold on to and complete in their lives this holiness which they have received" (Dogmatic Constitution on the Church, no. 40).

In the primitive Church all Christians were called "saints." Sanctity is a true dimension of man; it is his complete realization. To be within the creative plan of God we must strive for sanctity. A society without sanctity will be a society full of problems. Souls have a law of gravity: the will of God. Christ taught this well, and the Holy Spirit, through the Church, has made it a marvelous way of life. Sanctity is the qualification, the program and the desire of every Christian. "The Church needs sanctity" (Paul VI, September 18, 1974).

In order to reach sanctity it is necessary to overcome sin. St. Paul tells his Christians that "it is God's will that you grow in holiness." He also tells them what they must do to grow: "That you abstain from immorality, that each one of you know how to control his own body in holiness and honor, not in the passion of lust like the heathen who do not know God; that no man transgress his brother in this matter" (1 Thessalonians 4:3-6).

The foundation of holiness is our ability to accept the will of God. God seeks us but does not impose His friendship. Holiness is the result of a friendly meeting between the salvific will of God and our obedient will. This marvelous meeting takes place in the presence of the Holy Spirit. He helps us to choose the way of perfect love. Holiness is the greatest of His gifts.

Sanctity also means being immersed in the Church. The Church is the visible manifestation of Christ; it is His Body. The Church is the dwelling place of the Holy Spirit. In the Church we break the bread of life; we find the light of salvation. The Church is holy and thus she sanctifies. We participate in and receive the death and resurrection of Christ in the Church. The goal of the Church is to lead us to God.

PASTORAL REFLECTIONS

1. *To achieve holiness it is useful to know how others did so.* The study of man, no matter under what aspect, is always most interesting. The saints are particular persons who can teach us many interesting things. Most important of all, they tell us it is possible to do the will of God here on earth. The Church chooses and honors some of these experts in heavenly things to encourage and enlighten us.

2. *Holiness is a question of courage.* Faith calls for coherence in thought and action. The Gospels teach us charity, love, goodness and humility, and yet there is much selfishness, prejudice, dishonesty and arrogance in our lives. We must not fear. Courage united to the power of God is the formula for holiness. Our desire and intention should be: "Lord, I want to go straight to You.

Everything that impedes this must be eliminated. If it is my friends, I will leave them. If it is material goods, I will distribute them. If it is my body, let it be destroyed."

3. *A Prayer.* Lord, I want an ideal as high as the mountains, as bright as the sun and as strong as love. I want a dream to live even if it is difficult, burdensome and trying. Lord, give me a goal to strive for even if it is far away. Make me see the purpose of my life; show me a point of arrival.

Lord, You are my ideal, my dream, my goal and my point of arrival. Through holiness I will reach You. You are the only source of life. Amen.

THIRD SUNDAY IN ORDINARY TIME

Demonstration and Communion in the Church

Readings: Isaiah 8:23-9:3
1 Corinthians 1:10-13, 17
Matthew 4:12-23

Demonstrations, insubordinations and separations have always been part of the Church's history. Already in the times of St. Paul there were various opinions and separations. Corinth was a port city and certainly not an easy setting for a small Christian community. The community broke into four groups: those faithful to Paul, those faithful to Peter, those who followed Apollo, and those who wanted to follow Christ in their own way. Saint Paul immediately condemned this situation and offered the remedy: "For it has been reported to me by Chloe's people that there is quarreling among you, my brethren. What I mean is that each of you says, 'I belong to Paul' or, 'I belong to Apollos,' or 'I belong to Cephas' or, 'I belong to Christ.' Is Christ divided? Was Paul crucified for you? Or were you baptized in the name of Paul?...

Christ did not send me to baptize but to preach the gospel—not with eloquent 'wisdom,' lest the cross of Christ be emptied of its power" (cf. Second Reading).

Any and every division can be overcome if Christ is the basis of the union. Christ's purpose is to bring all things together (cf. Ephesians 1:10). The love of Christ is the force which opposes pride, hate and egoism. The fact that we are baptized in Christ means we belong to Him and that He is the exclusive Head of all.

The citizens of Corinth thought well of their cultural sufficiency. There was a tendency among some of them to do away with the passion and death of Christ and to give importance only to the Incarnation. Paul reminded them that he spoke only of Jesus Christ and Him crucified. Salvation does not come through us but from Him. The knowledge we have of God does not come from our sense of religion but from Christ who suffered and died on the cross for us. If we do not accept salvation as a gift coming from Christ on the cross, we are without faith. Faith is much more than an eloquent reasoning ability. The tendency to do away with the cross in order to make Christianity more acceptable is nothing more than to do away with Christ's entire message.

In order to unite the forces at Corinth, Paul refers to the Gospels. That which constitutes a Church is the faith which unites it. The basis of union is Christ and Christ is in the Gospels. "True religion is listening to and observing that mysterious yet clear voice which once said: 'He is my beloved Son. On him my favor rests, hear him' " (Paul VI, August 28, 1974). Does this mean there can be no personal initiative, no ecclesiastical pluralism? The Church can be compared to an orchestra which has many different instruments, yet all are united to produce one melody, the truth of Christ. As the faithful, as individual members of the People of God, we are all united and important. The value of an individual is his ability to associate with others in a collective effort.

PASTORAL REFLECTIONS

1. *We must find our unity in the Church, for the Church.* When one accepts Christ it is almost instinctive to feel and enjoy the Church. After his conversion André Frossard said: "I now feel the truth of every last detail of the Church's teachings." The Church is both a sign and the means of our union with God and with men. Christ gave His life to start the reality of the Church. Our task is to enlarge it, not to destroy it by divisions. An old African proverb says: "No one throws away the milk of a mother."

2. *The Church is a source of social strength.* The familiar saying is: "United we stand, divided we fall." The various organs and parts of our body can function only if they are united to the whole body. Pope John XXIII exhorted: "Not division, but peace; not egoism, but charity; not lies, but truth; not depression, but the triumph of light, purity, and mutual respect. This should be our witness now and forever."

3. *Every Christian will be in communion with the Church when he has a sense of Tradition.* In a certain sense, Tradition is more important than Scripture; it is more vast, and Scripture comes from Tradition. Experience teaches us that those who have abandoned the practical suggestions of Tradition and accepted only Scripture have ended in a vast diversity of opinion and in practice have destroyed truth. We must not abandon Tradition; it is full of practical suggestions for an authentic Christian life.

FOURTH SUNDAY IN ORDINARY TIME

The Dynamics of the Beatitudes

Readings: Zephaniah 2:3; 3:12-13
1 Corinthians 1:26-31
Matthew 5:1-12

At the peak of His apostolic life Christ revealed His challenging program of the beatitudes. It is a thoroughly different mentality; a completely new way of evaluating life: "Blest are the meek, the poor, the abused."

Christ went up to the mountainside to teach His disciples the beatitudes. Most of the great revelations come from an elevated place; for the Hebrews this "signified the importance and sanctity of the precepts" (St. Augustine).

We can summarize the meaning of the beatitudes in the words of St. Gregory the Great: "They are the eight steps to perfection." The beatitudes complete the commandments. The commandments are the moral laws which God has given to His creatures; the beatitudes are the moral laws God has given to His adopted children. The commandments are man's ethical hygiene; the beatitudes are the Christian's spiritual hygiene. The commandments are laws to protect us from evil; the beatitudes are laws to produce good—the "Magna Charta" of charity and sanctity.

Blest are the poor. It might be more correct to understand "poor" as "humble"; nevertheless, let us consider the literal sense. The person who is able to give the proper value to material things, to use them and not abuse them, is indeed happy. The very society in which we live desires things for us. Those who have everything are happy, and those who do not are unhappy—at least this is the way the advertisements put it. "There are more unhappy people for the lack of unnecessary things than there are for the lack of necessary things" (Fr. De La Lazere). This mentality must be changed. We must return to the proper use of things, and not make them the purpose of our lives, if we want to be part of God's people.

Blest are the sorrowing; they shall be consoled. Suffering is not to be eliminated from our lives at any cost; it has its proper place in our life. Christ died on a cross which was not to His liking. Human suffering can be physical, psychological or moral. Why do we suffer? Through suffering man learns to live; tears help man to see better.

Suffering ennobles man and makes him worthy of life. The storm uproots the small plant, but strengthens the roots of the solid oak.

Suffering is the school of sanctity; it is part of love. Man sees God well through his tears. There is only one way to glorification and eternal consolation—suffering.

Blest are the lowly. The meek person is like a sweet-smelling flower among a bunch of weeds. The meek do not get excited over every little thing. If they make a mistake, they simply begin over again. Criticism does not depress them. Meekness is like the earth: we all tramp on it, yet it supports each one of us. It is like bread: it is eaten by everyone, and it nourishes us. The meek person knows how to win and how to lose.

God prefers and dwells in the meek. The meek are strengthened by grace, and they have always dominated history without a lot of fanfare.

Blest are they who hunger and thirst for holiness; they shall have their fill. Holiness or justice, in the Biblical sense, is the peak of all virtues; it regulates our relationship with God. What we have cannot really satisfy us, but what we can become through virtue can fill our hearts. The story of our salvation is an invitation to virtue. We must make room for God in our lives as He alone can satisfy our hunger and quench our thirst.

Blest are they who show mercy; mercy shall be theirs. If we want to save our life, we must be ready to offer it. If we want to be loved, we must be merciful. We receive what we give; the hundredfold which returns to us depends on what we invest. To be the object of hatred is a frightful experience, but to hate without pardon is infernal. The happiness of love is found in an abundance of mercy.

Blest are the single-hearted, for they shall see God. In the Biblical sense, the heart is the center of our personality. To be single-hearted means to be motivated by a single intention, namely the love of God. The single-hearted sees and does everything in relation to God. To live twenty years or a hundred and twenty years is of little importance. What counts is to live in love with God. Dostoevski says: "Man lives between two abysses," and history teaches us that innocence and integrity always dominate (cf. *Brothers Karamazov*). When we have various and conflicting intentions in what we do, we become frustrated, inhibited, and no one understands us.

Blest too are the peacemakers. Peace should be the foundation of our relation with our society. Peace is such a tremendous good that no sacrifice should be too great to obtain it. The Church has always made every effort to spread peace. Since Vatican II the Church has undertaken the task to be the herald of peace. Christ's love for the world is peace; it is our duty as Christians to spread this love throughout the world.

Blest are those persecuted for holiness. Suffering, abuse or persecution is a consequence of doing good. The honest person, the one who does good, is detested by those who do evil because his way of living is a reprimand to theirs. If we intend to do good, we must be ready to accept criticism and constant refusal.

PASTORAL REFLECTIONS

1. The true Christian accepts and lives the beatitudes. We should pray with St. Ambrose: "Jesus, teach me the harmony of the beatitudes." The beatitudes must be part of our way of life, not something we do occasionally or at certain times.

2. *The fullness of the Christian life consists in carrying out this program.* The way Christ has harmonized contradicting elements in His program of the beatitudes is indeed marvelous: pain and joy; defeat and victory; humiliation and triumph; rejected by others, chosen by God. There is no abyss between the two extremities: time and eternity; they form a single unit. Living the beatitudes makes the Christian full and rich.

3. *True happiness can be found in the beatitudes.* We can consider the beatitudes as the eight notes of a hymn of joy. Once we have absorbed and fully trust

these eight ways of being blessed, we will have the key to happiness. There is a book entitled *A Right To Be Merry*. It is true, we all have a right to be happy, and now we know how to be happy.

FIFTH SUNDAY IN ORDINARY TIME

The Apostolic Commitment of the People of God

Readings: Isaiah 58:7-10
1 Corinthians 2:1-5
Matthew 5:13-16

The program of the beatitudes is not exclusive for the apostles; it is intended for all of God's people. It is their task to make it known throughout the world. Every Christian is an apostle. Christ was speaking to each one of us when He said: "You are the salt of the earth. But what if salt has lost its taste, shall its saltiness be restored? It is no longer good for anything except to be thrown out and trodden under foot by men. You are the light of the world. A city set on a hill cannot be hid. Nor do men light a lamp and put it under a bushel, but on a stand and it gives light to all in the house. Let your light so shine before men, that they may see your good works and give glory to your Father who is in Heaven" (Third Reading).

The apostolate is an organic necessity of the Christian vocation. The Christian passes from the natural to the supernatural and then on to action. The apostolate of the layman is not a theory but a reality, not a right but a duty. Vatican II teaches us that the Church is not just a clerical society but also a lay society. There is the priesthood and the laity, two separate realities united by the same Spirit for the universal apostolic action of the Church of God (cf. Dogmatic Constitution on the Church, no. 31).

Isaiah spoke of the hungry, the outcast and the oppressed, those who lack the material and spiritual necessities of life (cf. First Reading). These people still exist. The 93 articles of the Pastoral Constitution on the Church in the Modern World are a very clear invitation and exhortation to "dedicate ourselves to our fellowman and his organizations in order to animate them with the authentic spirit of Christ" (cf. Paul VI, July 8, 1974). The laity are the necessary "bridge" between the ecclesiastical and secular communities.

What means do the laity have to achieve their task? Today's liturgy gives us four: impede sin, defend the truth, witness to our salvation and trust in Christ.

To be the "salt of the earth" means to protect man from corruption. The ancient Hebrews considered salt as the symbol of purifying energy because of its caustic property. It eliminates anything that deteriorates or corrupts. They put salt on their sacrificial animals to conserve them and to make them more worthy (cf. Leviticus 2:13). The apostle must be ready to fight evil, the source of disruption and social abnormality. The apostle must fight every form of evil: social injustice, prejudice, pornography, hatred, untruth, etc. Evil gets the upper hand when we Christians do nothing.

The apostle must enlighten others with the light of the Gospels. The Word of God is necessary for every individual, for every family and for society. There is a proportion between lack of truth and lack of civilization. The Gospels are not just words. They are life. They are light. They are rebirth. They are salvation. The history of man is bright and clear when seen in the light of the Gospels. The apostle brings the light of the Word of God to the world so that it can grow and bear fruit.

If the apostle does not live and witness what he believes, his efforts will be in vain. Scientific truths are demonstrated; religious truths are witnessed. Actions speak louder than words. Knowledge convinces the intellect, but example convinces the will. Example is the best way to show that what we say is possible. This is what Ghandi, the great mystic and sociologist, meant when he said: "Preach with your life, like the rose which does not speak but perfumes its entire surrounding; even the blind person is aware of its presence."

Christ's death on the cross is our guarantee that God loves us. We can experience God's love by contemplating Christ crucified. United to the cross we can learn to love others in the midst of contradiction and delusion. Our contribution to society depends on our connection with the cross (cf. Second Reading).

PASTORAL REFLECTIONS

1. *The Holy Father invites us to action.* "Once we have overcome the period of doubt, uncertainty and laziness, we should feel the need to build a new society based on Christian ideals. We must feel the joy of working together, generously, in real friendship. As Christians, we are all capable of courageous activity. The world today needs a moral and religious dimension which can generate hope. I extend a personal invitation to everyone who is proud of his Christian beliefs, to take part in the task of spreading the kingdom of Christ" (Paul VI, November 18, 1973).

2. *The apostle must be ready to forget himself, to suffer and be humiliated.* This requires an enormous capacity for love. God does not reward on the basis of quantity or results. What is fundamental is the intention. Our capacity for apostolic work depends on our ability to love.

3. *A Christian preference: the poor.* "I have knocked at your door. I need a place to rest and to warm myself. Why do you refuse me? Open, brother! Why do you ask me if I come from Africa, or from America, or from Asia or from Europe? Open, brother! Why do you ask me how long my nose is, how thick my lips are, or what color my skin is? Open, brother! I am not a Negro, I am not an Indian, I am not an Asiatic nor a White. I am

simply a man. Open, brother! Open your heart, because I am a man of all times, a man of all places, I am a man like you" (Renè Philombe, Cameroun).

SIXTH SUNDAY IN ORDINARY TIME

Christ, the Law, and Love

Readings: Sirach 15:15-20
1 Corinthians 2:6-10
Matthew 5:17-37

The First and Third Readings of today's liturgy are an open invitation to reflect on the law and the innovations which Christ brought.

The name Yahweh, the proper, personal name for God, appears some 6,800 times in the Old Testament. We know its meaning: "I am who am" or "He who works with power and wisdom." The laws we find in nature reflect this power and wisdom.

The wisdom of God is expressed in various ways: the moral laws "written in the hearts of man," the positive laws of man suggested by God and the positive laws of God given directly by God.

In a certain sense our conscience is part of natural law; it has an important role in our moral lives. Our conscience, considering the directives of positive law, evaluates our actions. If the conscience is false or has been erroneously formed, it can no longer distinguish between good and evil.

In order not to err in this important matter, we have received from God human and divine positive laws. Human laws are the rule for good actions, and divine laws are the force to act well.

The divine law sustains us. It is an expression of God's infinite goodness. Its goal is our spiritual good. It corresponds to the longings of our hearts.

The law God gave to the Hebrew people with time became a simple external observance, a list of precepts.

Christ's mission was to re-establish the value of this law. Positive law must become an interior choice, a personal intention. Christ added a new dimension—love.

The most important dimension of the law is its interior aspect. Jesus came to complete the law. He described this in detail: it is not enough simply not to kill; we must not hold a grudge against anyone. It is not enough simply not to commit adultery; we must not have evil desires. External washing is not sufficient; we must be interiorly purified. External observance is not enough; there must be an interior adherence. The spirit of the law is important, not the letter only.

Christ explained the reason for this interior dimension. God is present in each and every human being. At times we have an excellent reasoning process to justify our prejudices, our aloofness, our lack of interest, yet God is present in those we despise.

In a certain sense there is only one law—the law of love with its two aspects: love of God and love of man. "The love of God and brotherhood of man is a short and simple expression of one law" (George H. Boldt, U.S. Federal Judge).

PASTORAL REFLECTIONS

1. *The law is an instrument of life.* If we eliminate every law, we are condemned to mental and operative nihilism. We cannot call the sun a balloon or the moon a pumpkin, nor can we say that two plus two is five, nor can we assert that Julius Caesar was a classmate of Napoleon. Traffic laws are for our own safety and security. The purpose of divine law is not so much to define ethical limits as to provide us with sure norms for doing good. God is the origin of virtue and He invites us to perfection through the law. A civil state cannot exist without laws. In the same way religion cannot exist without love for the law.

2. *There is no contradiction between love and action,* between freedom and operative choice. There are

rules in the New Testament (cf. 1 Corinthians 7:10); however, their purpose is not authoritarianism but an indication of new areas where we can live and exercise our Christian love. Christ said: "He who obeys the commandments he has from me is the man who loves me" (John 14:21). "Love is demonstrated by actions" (St. Gregory the Great). There is respect for our freedom; we can choose the way in which we want to express our love. St. Augustine said: "Love and do what you like."

3. *The Christian notion of authority-obedience.* He who gives orders must be in the service of the Word and of love. He who obeys must be capable of listening to the Word, so as not to invalidate his own program of love. The greater the authority, the greater the charity, and the greater the charity, the greater the obedience.

SEVENTH SUNDAY IN ORDINARY TIME

Love and Enemies

> Readings: Leviticus 19:1-2, 17-18
> 1 Corinthians 3:16-23
> Matthew 5:38-48

Surely one of the more difficult aspects of Christ's teaching is to love those who harm us.

As Christians we are called to be like our heavenly Father, who loves all men, even those who hate Him. We cannot be like God in His essence. God is wisdom, we are ignorance. God is omnipotence, we are weakness. God is eternal, we are limited in time. We can, however, imitate God in His actions. Today's liturgy suggests a very practical aspect for this imitation: love your enemies (cf. Third Reading). Christ has given us an excellent example.

Without faith and love of God, it is impossible to love our enemies. An episode in the life of Jonah the prophet is pertinent. Jonah became quite angry over the fact that God forgave the people of Nineveh after he had preached fire and brimstone. Pouting he left the city and sat down to rest. The Lord provided a gourd plant to give Jonah shade but the next day the plant dried up. Exasperatedly shaking his fist towards the sky, Jonah cried: "I would be better off dead than alive."

God answered: "You are concerned over the plant which cost you no labor and which you did not raise. It came up in one night, and in one night it perished. And should I not be concerned over Nineveh, the great city, in which there are more than a hundred and twenty thousand persons who cannot distinguish their right hand from their left, not to mention the cattle?" (cf. Jonah 4)

We must be kind to each person, no matter what his ethics are; every human being is God's property. This is true even when man is in sin. "The value of a soul, whether it be of an imbecile or of an outlaw, of a spy or of a traitor, is worth more than all the riches of the earth put together" (Leon Bloy). Some of St. Augustine's friends hinted that he took advantage of God's mercy. He replied: "The mercy which saved me, calling me from sin to grace, is the very same mercy which has kept you from falling from grace into sin."

When someone points out our shortcomings or defects we usually try to explain why we do certain things or to find some sort of justification. We make every effort to make others understand us. This same mechanism should be useful in carrying out the difficult precept of love of enemies. "Do not be upset if others do not understand you, but if you can no longer understand others, then it is time to worry" (Paul Claudel).

Jesus taught us to look at ourselves: "First take the log out of your own eye, and then you will see clearly to take the speck out of your brother's eye" (Matthew 7:5). There is an Oriental proverb which says: "Before you criticize the dirt in the city, clean your own house." Even if we have made much progress along the way of perfection, when we feel justified in judging and punishing others we should recall the negative moments of our past.

If we are surrounded by people of our choice and liking, there will be less occasion to grow in virtue. Saint Benedict insisted on community life, because the reciprocal contact with the defects and psychological quirks of others is an excellent occasion to grow in charity.

PASTORAL REFLECTIONS

1. *The life of a Christian is a contest of love.* We are winners in this contest, because, as Christ said, "whoever loses his life for my sake will find it" (Matthew 16:25). Christian love grows and multiplies when it is generously given to everyone. If we reflect for a moment, we can see that we have experienced this contest of love. I help someone, and God makes me happy. I forgive another, and God forgets my defects, even permits me to be praised. I bear with a difficult character, and God puts up with me and stays near me. I make an effort to be of service to another, and God overwhelms me with unexpected favors. We can never really get ahead of God in this contest, and at the same time we never lose. Recall the words of the Lord who said: "It is more blessed to give than to receive" (Acts 20:35).

2. *A code of spiritual brotherhood.* Each morning take Jesus "meek and humble of heart" as your model. Keep calm in body and soul, even when left alone or mistreated. Determine objectively just what you can do for others. Foresee the situation where more self-control will be needed. Be positive when speaking of others. Accept those you consider impossible. Be sociable. A smile, a greeting may mean a lot to someone in difficulty. Discuss your good qualities only with yourself. If it is necessary to correct someone, do so positively. Seek forgiveness when you have hurt another.

3. *"It is impossible to forget an offense."* Our reflection on love and enemies would not be complete if we do not consider this objection. Good and evil stem from the will, not from our sentiments or psychological reactions. Memory is a faculty of the intellect, not of the will.

Consequently, to remember an offense or feel its sting is not an act of the will. We do evil when the will enters and wants revenge.

EIGHTH SUNDAY IN ORDINARY TIME

Divine Fidelity and Human Trust

Readings: Isaiah 49:14-15
1 Corinthians 4:1-5
Matthew 6:24-34

God is love (cf. 1 John 4:8) and this love is eternal and faithful. In the biblical sense "divine fidelity" means that God continues to love His creatures even when they turn away from Him. "Can a woman forget her sucking child, that she should have no compassion on the son of her womb? Even these may forget yet I will not forget you" (cf. First Reading).

The promise is very nice, but reality seems to be something else. People die of starvation. We are lonely. Every day we read about some new disaster, some more senseless suffering. How can we reconcile the harsh reality with the biblical promise? Love respects, it does not impose itself. Sunlight will enter a room only if we open the blinds. Our free will is the maximum demonstration of God's immense love for us. God does not impose a predetermined plan on us. Through His love He offers, helps, stimulates us to cooperate with Him. Love between two persons on a natural level is capable of producing new energies, new life. There should be no limit to what we can do when our love meets and responds to God's love for us. There is a certain connection between God's fidelity and our trust, between God's goodness and our free will. "Know therefore that the Lord your God is God, the faithful God who keeps covenant and steadfast love with those who love him and keep his commandments, to a thousand generations" (Deuteronomy 7:9).

The key to the problem of harsh reality and God's promises is man's free will. Rather than cooperate with God, that is, trust Him, man tends to put more faith in what he can produce (cf. Third Reading). God's power, divine Providence is conditioned by man's cooperation or by man's weakness, that is, by man's bad use of his free will. In other words, our nobility as free creatures can also be our downfall.

God insists that He loves us. Why then do we have to suffer so much? It is certain that God loves us. He also respects our free will and finite nature. Is it true that all suffering is a negative experience? Suffering helps us to redimension our spirit and seek supernatural good. In the pain of solitude we find the riches of dialogue with God.

Frequently, human suffering, which seems to contradict divine Providence, has a supernatural significance. To trust blindly is certainly not easy for man, and frequently it is in this difficult moment that God intervenes. Peter was an experienced fisherman. It was against his principles to cast his nets the way Christ wanted him to (cf. Luke 5:1-11). It was not easy for the ten lepers to go to show themselves to the priests knowing they were not yet made clean (cf. Luke 17:11-15). Frequently when God seems to be very far away is the very moment He is about to do something special for us.

God helps us overcome our sufferings, this is an indication of His love for us, He will never try us beyond our strength (cf. 1 Corinthians 10:13; Hebrews 2:18). God expresses His love for us through His fidelity; we must learn to increase our trust in God.

PASTORAL REFLECTIONS

1. *Trust in God, especially when everything seems to go wrong.* When we feel useless, empty, incapable of doing anything, this is the moment when God is about to fill us with His love. We all have moments when we no longer trust anything or anyone. These are the moments

to prove our fidelity. A shadow always indicates the presence of light; our misery is always invaded by God's goodness.

2. When we are misunderstood, rashly judged, or ill-treated by others, it is always consoling to know that *God sees us.* "He will bring to light what is hidden in darkness and manifest the intentions of hearts. At that time, everyone will receive his praise from God" (cf. Second Reading). If others refuse us, we have a good reason to get closer to God. Men judge appearances, but God sees in the heart.

3. *It is impossible to trust without prayer.* When we seek help we express our trust and this is prayer (cf. Matthew 8:25). If we can pray in the midst of our sufferings, we will not lose heart. Even if the whole world seems to collapse, if we pray we have nothing to fear. "What difference does it make if the future is cloudy? Be with me and protect me for today" (St. Theresa of the Child Jesus). We can make Cardinal Newman's prayer ours: "Lord, protect me. I do not ask to know the future; I am satisfied to reach You step by step."

NINTH SUNDAY IN ORDINARY TIME

The Essence of Christian Life

Readings: Deuteronomy 11:18, 26-28
Romans 3:21-25, 28
Matthew 7:21-27

Obedience to God will be rewarded. He who does the will of the Father will enter the kingdom of God (cf. First and Third Readings).

The greatness of man is not in his intellectual ability, but in his will through which he gives a value to external objects. The dynamic message of Christ must be inserted in this transcendental property of the will. All the authors of the New Testament stress this in various ways.

Matthew used the parable of the silver pieces to prepare us for the fact that we will be judged on the basis of our operative love in relation to others (cf. Matthew 25:14-30). The parable of the Good Samaritan is Luke's way of telling us that we must do good (cf. Luke 10:30-38). James is famous for his teaching on faith and good works (cf. James 2:14-26). Peter tells us to overcome evil by doing good (cf. 1 Peter 2:15). John shows us how love of God and of neighbor are, dynamically, the same thing (cf. John 15:8-9). And Paul constantly stresses the evident reality that we cannot be friends of God unless we obey His commandments. The Gospels make a clear distinction between those who hear the Word of God (intellectual activity) and those who live the Word of God (activity of the will).

"Faith that does nothing in practice is thoroughly lifeless" (James 2:17). Faith without works is like a cloud that does not give rain, like a bud that does not bloom, like a spark that does not ignite. Likewise, works without faith have no religious content. They are like a beautiful car without a motor. Man in his essential nature is intellect and will; the essence of a Christian is faith and action. In order to reach full maturity in Christ St. Paul tells us we must "profess the truth in love" (Ephesians 4:15).

It might be useful to reconsider briefly the various components of an act of the will. Man, and much more the Christian, must frequently choose. His ideal is to choose what is good. To give the proper value to things, we need some reference criterion—the Word of God and the teaching of the Church. The first phase of an act of the will is the evaluation of the various activities in relation to the accepted criterion. Then there is the decision, the actual choice. There is, necessarily, some value attached to this choice; otherwise, it is not the fruit of the will. The will has a natural tendency towards what is good (cf. St. Thomas I-II, 9) or at least that which is seen as good. The third phase is to relate these partial or finite goods to the Highest Good. In this moment the human free will has reached its maximum activity. This is the moment in which the real Christian is distinguished from the person who is simply registered as Christian.

PASTORAL REFLECTIONS

1. *Christianity is the religion of virtues.* God invites us to do good, but He does not make us do it. When God created man He gave him a will, intelligence and wisdom. He then placed before man life and death (cf. Deuteronomy 30:10). Consequently, man can choose the way of life and live forever, or the way of death and be an eternal failure. Sanctity is simply choosing the way of what is good.

2. *Sanctity is the fruit of the will united to the grace of God.* To achieve sanctity is not a question of time. It is a question of love, dynamic love. The little boy in front of the show window of a toy store contemplates many things he would like to have. At a certain point he must decide what he wants, go into the store and buy it. Immediately after his conversion Paul asked: "What is it that I must do?" (Acts 22:9) In the *Imitation of Christ* we read: "You will progress in virtue in proportion to your ability to will." Sanctity is not beautiful music to be enjoyed passively; it is a program which requires energy and conviction.

3. *We must not get discouraged if we do not succeed as we would like to.* Conversion is not an instant or flash of lightning; it is a constant way of life. Sanctity is not a sudden deviation from evil towards good; it is orienting everything towards the Absolute Good. We must keep our ideals in mind at all times if we intend to fulfill them. In ancient times the hero was the man who fought until he died. The true Christian is the person who loves and works up to the very end of his earthly existence (cf. Matthew 10:22).

TENTH SUNDAY IN ORDINARY TIME

The Mercy of God

> Readings: Hosea 6:3-6
> Romans 4:18-25
> Matthew 9:9-13

Our efforts, activity and cooperation with God have a certain stability because God, in His infinite love, is ready to forgive our weaknesses. "And as he [Jesus] sat at table in the house, many tax collectors and sinners came and sat down with Jesus and his disciples. And when the Pharisees saw this, they said to his disciples: 'Why does your teacher eat with tax collectors and sinners?' But when he heard it, he said: 'I came not to call the righteous, but sinners' " (cf. Third Reading).

To better appreciate the value of God's mercy, it is necessary to understand just what sin is.

It does not take much reflection to realize that evil is not outside or around us; it is within us. St. Paul dedicates chapter seven of his letter to the Romans to this interior struggle between the intellectual desire of what is good and the tendency towards evil due to our weak nature. In a certain sense it is impossible to list all the sins man could commit, and then there are the sins of omission. Jesus stressed the interior element of sin when He said: "Everyone who looks at a woman lustfully has already committed adultery with her" (Matthew 5:28). The humiliating reality is: we are all sinners.

St. Paul says we are weak flesh sold into the slavery of sin (cf. Romans 7:14). Christ is the High Priest "without sin" who destroys our sins. He has offered Himself in sacrifice to the Father for our sins. Our Redemption from sin is not a single act fixed in time; it is constantly renewed. God's mercy fills the past, the present and the future.

Through the ages this marvelous theme of God's mercy has been treated by all eminent Christian writers.

Some have written: "God's benevolence is without limit. All our sins together will never surpass God's love, just as our illness cannot overwhelm the expertise of the doctor" (St. Cyril of Jerusalem). "When men give materially, they have less; but God is enriched when He forgives; because only in this way does His love become mercy" (St. Lucy Filippini). "I believe that God is more tender than a mother. A mother is always ready to forgive the faults of her child. God does the same for us; we are in His merciful care" (St. Theresa of the Child Jesus).

PASTORAL REFLECTIONS

1. *"In God we trust."* The worst possible situation for man is that absolute depression in which he refuses God's mercy. Once a penitent went to Blessed Placido Riccardi saying he had committed every possible sin. Placido replied: "The fact that you are here means that there is at least one sin you did not commit, namely, to doubt God's mercy." Rather than just a motto printed on coins, let us make "In God we trust" our way of life.

2. *Christ's crucifixion is the basis of our trust.* "Jesus took upon Himself all the sins of the entire world. God could have saved man in an easier way. However, to show the magnitude of His love, He chose the cross. The cross is our justice. The cross is our salvation. The cross reveals God's infinite love for us. Never forget this; in fact, tell the whole world about it" (Paul VI, April 12, 1974).

3. *A Prayer.*

Lord, do not abandon me, even if I deserve it.
Do not abandon me, even if I fail frequently.
Do not lose patience with me.
Help me to take the proper advantage of Your mercy.
You know how weak I am, understand me!
You know that the evil forces try to keep me from You.
Forgive me Lord, always.
Forgive all my weakness, whatever wrong I do.
Forgive and forget!
Forgive me and never abandon me!

ELEVENTH SUNDAY IN ORDINARY TIME

The Blood of Christ

> Readings: Exodus 19:2-6
> Romans 5:6-11
> Matthew 9:36; 10:8

The Second Reading of today's liturgy returns us to the theme of God's mercy: "While we were still sinners, Christ died for us."

Blood had a certain significance in the Old Testament Jewish ceremonies. It recalled the freedom from Egypt and protection from destruction. It also had a particular expiatory value. The high priest would enter the "Holy of Holies" with the blood of the sacrificed victims and offer it to obtain God's mercy for the people. The more significant use of blood was to renew the covenant between God and His people. During this ceremony blood was spattered in equal parts on the altar and on the people, while the high priest said: "This is the blood of the covenant which the Lord has made with you in accordance with all these words of his" (cf. Exodus 24:3-8).

It is logical that the authors of the New Testament envision the blood of Christ in this Old Testament mentality. Christ foretold His death three times (cf. Matthew 8:31, 9:31, 10:33). Then He waited for the moment of His supreme sacrifice when He would give His blood (cf. Luke 22:20). St. Clement of Alexandria frequently repeated: "The vine gives its wine as Christ gives His blood." "Jesus went up to Calvary and was wounded in order to give us His blood" (St. Anthony of Padua).

The reasons why the Redeemer shed His blood are those indicated in the Old Testament. In the New Testament, they take on a salvific dimension. Christ shed His blood, first of all, as an act of adoration to the Father. This was foreseen by the Psalmist (cf. Psalm 40:7) and later explained by John and Paul (cf. John 17; Philippians 2:6-11).

Christ offered His blood to glorify the Father. At the same time we benefit for our sins are expiated. In his letter to the Hebrews, St. Paul makes every effort to clarify this aspect of Christ's sacrifice. "He entered, taking not the blood of goats and calves but His own blood,...[He] offered himself without blemish to God, to purify your conscience from dead works to serve the living God" (Hebrews 9:12-14).

This purification also regards the Church: "Christ's whole body sweat blood to heal and restore the spiritual body of the Church" (St. Bonaventure, *The Mystical Life*, XIX, 2).

In the Hebrew mentality, contact with the blood of the victim was a way to communicate with God. Contact with blood saved them from slavery in Egypt (cf. Exodus 12). Sprinkled with blood, they renewed their covenant with God near Mt. Sinai (cf. Exodus 24:8). By repeating this same ceremony they would solemnly and publicly proclaim that they were God's people (cf. Numbers, chapters 8-10). The blood of Christ makes this covenant with God complete and universal. On Calvary the name of the Lord becomes "great among the nations, and in every place incense is offered to my name and a pure offering" (Malachi 1:11).

"You were slain and by your blood
> ransomed men for God

from every tribe and tongue and
> people and nation."

(Revelation 5:9)

PASTORAL REFLECTIONS

1. *The blood of Christ should circulate in our souls.* The science of biology tells us that there are billions of red and white blood cells circulating in our body. These cells bring food to the other body tissues and consequently our health depends on them. In a similar way we can say our sanctity depends on the mystical circula-

tion of Christ's blood in our souls. Through the blood of Christ we are freed from our sins and nourished along the way of perfection (cf. Hebrews 10:19-22).

2. *The blood of Christ is the life of the Church.* The Church is born from the blood of Christ; whatever good the Church does, it is in force of the blood of Christ. The Church is authentic when it leads us to Calvary, when it defends and appreciates the blood of Christ.

3. *The prayer of St. Catherine of Siena*: I hope and trust in the blood of the sacrificed Lamb; my sins will be forgiven, and I will receive grace. Even if all the sins of mankind were attributed to one person they would be like a drop in the ocean of mercy revealed on Calvary. Jesus, my soul desires to be bathed in Your blood. In Your blood there is mercy and clemency; in Your blood there is pity and justice. In Your blood my rigidness is dissolved. In Your blood the bitter things of life become sweet; the burdens become light. In Your blood virtue grows and matures; therefore, drown my soul so that I may achieve true virtue.

TWELFTH SUNDAY IN ORDINARY TIME

The Apostolate and Persecution

Readings: Jeremiah 20:10-13
Romans 5:12-15
Matthew 10:26-33

"The world, in its more negative sense, can be understood as humanity, that is, that part of humanity which refuses the light of Christ and lives in sin; that part of humanity which embraces principles of life that are contrary to God, the faith and the Gospels" (Paul VI, March 23, 1977). In this context we can understand how the history of man is a battle between good and evil. The Book of Revelation pictures it as a struggle between the angel and the dragon, between the ranks of Christ and the ranks of Satan, between the remaining faithful and the masses who are far from God. Christ frequently mentions similar opposites: sin and grace, light and darkness.

This battle at times becomes a tragedy in which the Christian apostle suffers. The First Reading of today's liturgy gives us an excellent example: Jeremiah was criticized, abused and despised. Christ said it would be so: "They will persecute you as they persecuted me" (John 15:20; Acts 9:15). St. Paul experienced the truth of this prophecy both in his body and his spirit (cf. Ephesians 3:8-21; Acts 20:18-23).

Can we give any explanation for this suffering? To establish and live any ideal is a struggle and consequently suffering. To love Christ, to defend His teaching and to spread the Good News is not easy. Every attempt to do good will be questioned by those who have different ideals. During His public life, Christ's teaching usually evoked anger and hatred.

Another partial reason is that the apostle should participate in the sufferings of Christ (cf. 1 Peter 1:6-9; 3:14; 4:1; Romans 5:3-5; John 15:20). Christ became victim for our sins and suffered to save us (cf. Isaiah 52, 53); the apostle continues this suffering to bring salvation to others.

The apostle "calls a spade a spade" and many people do not like this. Many apostles have been killed for this reason: "And he (Paul) spoke and disputed against the Hellenists; but they were seeking to kill him" (Acts 9:29). The list of fearless Christians who were put to death like John the Baptist (cf. Luke 1:15-17) and Stephen (cf. Acts 2:3-4) for speaking clearly is endless.

Another source of strife for the apostle stems from the fact that he must live in the world and not be part of its materialistic, hedonistic ways. To be a herald of the truth in the pragmatic world of today is not an easy task. If we denounce sin, we are pessimists. When we expound the goodness of the Lord, we avoid the issue. If we speak of social problems, we are politicians. If we speak of the future, we are utopian. If we look to the past, we are conservative. When we consider the present, we are existentialists and irresponsible. But we should not be surprised: "Go on your way; behold, I send you out as lambs in the midst of wolves" (Luke 10:3).

The sufferings of others in some situations seem to be locked in a vicious circle. Humanly speaking, there is apparently nothing that can relieve the suffering. Situations like this are very humiliating for the apostle. We are limited, and others suffer more than we do.

PASTORAL REFLECTIONS

1. *The apostle participates in the fertile suffering of the Church.* The Church is capable of giving life precisely because she suffers. Recalling the deaths of Saints Peter and Paul, St. Leo the Great said: "The Church is not diminished by persecutions; persecutions are the preparation for a new harvest. The seed must die before it produces new life. These two seeds, Peter and Paul, will be multiplied and their City will abound with apostles and martyrs. In spite of our sins we receive God's mercy through their merits" (Sermon 82).

2. Only in the perspective of salvation and benefit for the entire Mystical Body *can we understand innocent suffering.* "Constant, innocent suffering endured for love is what saves and redeems" (Paul VI, March 27, 1970). The Church appreciates the value of innocent suffering, and she invites those who suffer innocently to be apostles. "If all the Christians who suffer could be enlisted in the missionary apostolate, if all the hospitals, clinics and rest homes could become centers of mystical missionary activity, if all suffering could be offered to God in love, oh, what a marvelous effect it would have for the Church!" (Pope John XXIII)

3. *Apostolic suffering does not exclude happiness.* "Do not fear those who can deprive the body of life but cannot destroy the soul" (cf. Third Reading). The apostle

will find rest and consolation in his union with God. Happiness and suffering are two opposite experiences; in God they become complementary. When we are united to Christ and inserted in His missionary apostolate, suffering makes sense. It becomes love and joy: "I wrote you out of much affliction and anguish... to let you know the abundant love that I have for you" (2 Corinthians 2:4).

THIRTEENTH SUNDAY IN ORDINARY TIME

Hospitality

Readings: 2 Kings 4:8-11, 14-16
Romans 6:3-4, 8-11
Matthew 10:37-42

Christ was aware of the difficulties that await an apostle. As if to make things a bit easier for the apostle He promised rewards for those who receive His messengers. Even a cup of water will have its reward (cf. Third Reading).

The duty or custom of hospitality is rooted in the very early history of mankind. The tradition and legends from all parts of the world and all religions indicate the necessity to receive pilgrims, those who are unfortunate, or who have been exiled.

This is quite evident in the Old Testament. Abraham hosts the three men at Mambre (cf. Genesis 18:1-8). Laban goes out of his way to receive Abraham's servant (cf. Genesis 24:28-32). The prophet Elisha received extended hospitality from a woman of influence in Shunem (cf. First Reading). Hospitality is in the tradition of the Hebrew people. Always and everywhere they considered themselves to be God's guests. The promised land is God's property; they are the guests (cf. Leviticus 25:23). One of the preferred themes of the Psalms is recognition to God because He gave them hospitality in a fertile land. The Hebrew people had lived in foreign countries and had experienced the hardships of being outcasts; consequently, they appreciated hospitality (cf. Leviticus 19:33-37).

Christ gave considerable importance to hospitality. He mentions it indirectly in the parable of the Good Samaritan and the parable of the unexpected friend, in which the host woke up his neighbor to get something to eat for his friend. In his craftiness, the wily manager assures hospitality for himself. He who is humble and takes the lowest seat is sure to obtain future hospitality. Christ accepted hospitality frequently from people of all social classes. He was a guest of Matthew at Capharnaum, of Zaccheus at Jericho, of the two disciples at Emmaus. He stayed frequently and longer at the homes of Peter and Lazarus. In the early Church "to receive one's brethren" was a religious obligation, rendering one worthy of divine revelation (cf. Luke 24:29). Peter spent quite some time at the home of Simon in Jaffa, and at the home of Cornelius in Caesarea. After his escape from prison he stayed with Mark in Jerusalem. St. Paul had various foster homes, at Philippi the home of Lady Lydia, at Corinth he lived with Aquila and Priscilla, at Caesarea with Philip. While at Malta the governor Publius gave him lodging and all he needed to continue his journey (cf. Acts 28:2-10). The apostle is poor in spirit and exchanges the bread of truth for his daily bread. From the teachings of Christ and of the Church it is possible to draw up the following code of Christian hospitality:

1. Sincere interest, as the disciples at Emmaus had for Jesus and Lydia for Paul (cf. Luke 24:29; Acts 16:11-15).

2. Joyful service (cf. Luke 19:6; Acts 16:34; cf. 1 Peter 4:9).

3. Satisfying every need (cf. Acts 28:2-10).

4. Hospitality is a charism of the Holy Spirit to distribute the multiform grace of God (cf. 1 Peter 4:7-10).

5. Hospitality is based on faith, for every guest should be received as an angel of the Lord (cf. Hebrews 13:1-2), as Christ Himself (cf. Galatians 4:13-14).

6. Hospitality presupposes trust: "Take no gold, nor silver, nor copper in your belts, no bag for your journey, nor two tunics, nor sandals, nor a staff" (Matthew 10:9-10).

7. Hospitality is sincere, effective Christian charity (cf. 3 John 1:8) which imitates Christ who said: "Come to me all you who labor and are heavy laden, I will give you rest" (Matthew 11:28).

PASTORAL REFLECTIONS

1. *There is a great need in the world today of hospitality.* In more ancient times hospitality was part of the way of life. Perhaps it was due to the fact that there were more difficulties, and it was practically impossible for someone to remain completely isolated. Today living conditions are much different. But the fact remains, the lone traveler, the person far from his family rejoices when he is well received. Modern man is constantly immersed in a sea of people, forever doing things, and yet many of us feel very lonely, even in our own families. It is indeed a pleasant and consoling experience to be simply accepted for what we are, just an ordinary human being.

2. *The life of an apostle should be a simple life.* The apostle, the traveler, the guest should not be pretentious. St. Paul and St. Francis of Assisi are excellent examples. The guest should make every attempt to adapt to the situation and not make a burden of himself. Jesus was not always received well (cf. John 1:11; Luke 9:58); the apostle should not be surprised if the same happens to him.

3. *A prayer.*

Lord, be merciful to those I do not know. Help me to accept them as coming from You. Help me to be open, kind, hospitable and enthusiastic. I want my home to be a haven of rest and happiness for others. Lord, I want to experience joy in meeting others and sadness when they leave. I want to be able to receive others as I hope to be received one day by You.

FOURTEENTH SUNDAY IN ORDINARY TIME

The Theology of Humility

Readings: Zechariah 9:9-10
Romans 8:9, 11-13
Matthew 11:25-30

Humility is a Christian reality. "Father, Lord of heaven and earth, to you I offer praise, for what you have hidden from the learned and the clever you have revealed to the merest children" (Third Reading).

Humility is also a human reality. What is the value of the human body? A slight deformation in a single brain lobe is sufficient to cause idiocy. A grain of dust in an eye and we no longer see. A tiny hole in the intestines can cause death. The physiology of many animals is much superior. The kestrel can see a thousand times better than man. This small hack can spot an insect on the ground from an altitude of 600 yards and can fly at speeds up to 70 m.p.h. Intellectually, man is also limited; the more we understand, the more there is to understand.

On the supernatural level humility is a necessity. The Pharisee who boasted about what he did for God was condemned by Christ (cf. Luke 18:9-14). When we are full of ourselves there is no room for anyone else, not even for God. The proud and haughty person is lonely and suspects everyone. "The Lord feeds the lambs, not the wolves" (St. John Chrysostom).

Humility is the entrance to the kingdom of God. "To enter the kingdom of heaven you must become like children" (cf. Mark 10:14). We speak of children; the term used in the ancient Greek text indicates mere infants (cf. Luke 18:15). We must become small to enter God's kingdom.

God entered man's world in complete humility (cf. Philippians 2:7); man will enter God's world through the same door. Our capacity to receive grace is directly proportional to our humility; like a well, the deeper it is, the more water it can hold.

Humility is the foundation of every virtue and the criterion to judge sanctity. Tradition has it that once in Rome, during the time of St. Philip Neri, there was a lady with the reputation of a saint. The Pope wanted some firsthand information. He called Philip and asked him to look into this matter. On his way to the lady's home, Philip managed to cover his shoes with mud. When the famous lady received him he simply asked her to clean his shoes. Hurt and raging she left the room without saying a word. Later he informed the Pope: "That lady cannot be a saint; she is not humble." St. Bernard describes sanctity as a house: the walls are justice, fortitude, temperance and prudence; the roof is patience; the windows, prayer; the door, fear of God. The owner is the intellect; the lady, the will; the children, good works; the servants, the senses; the guests, the Father, the Son and the Holy Spirit. The foundation of this marvelous house is humility. "Where there is humility, there is obedience, cooperation and love; where there is humility, there is hope and sanctity" (Paul VI, February 5, 1975).

PASTORAL REFLECTIONS

1. *Pride and arrogance are at the root of all social evils.* "When man is dominated by pride and arrogance he makes himself the only criterion with which he evaluates life. He is the purpose of his life and others are to be used. Egoism can produce a certain culture and

much activity which seems to satisfy, but love is missing. Pride robs love of its universality, of its disinterestedness, its capacity to understand and relieve the sufferings of others" (Paul VI, January 5, 1975).

2. *Humility is the beginning of greatness.* Only Christian teaching can explain the apparent contradictions of many great people. For example: Mary, the Mother of God, passed as a simple housewife in Nazareth. The humility of the saints is well known to everyone. On December 14, 1976, Pope Paul VI celebrated Mass for the unity of the Churches. On leaving the Sistine Chapel the Holy Father stopped and knelt before Melitone, the Archbishop of Calcedonia, and kissed his feet. Later a news reporter from Athens said: "Only a great man can humble himself in this way."

3. *The program for humility of Charles de Foucauld.* "My desire, my mission: to go unknown through the world, like a traveler in the night; to pass silently and like Jesus of Nazareth, to be poor and humble. I want to do good silently without receiving any credit from others. I want to immolate myself in silence, without any resistance, imitating Jesus on the cross" (Charles de Foucauld, May 17, 1904).

FIFTEENTH SUNDAY IN ORDINARY TIME

Evangelization and the Word of God

Readings: Isaiah 55:10-11
Romans 8:18-23
Matthew 13:1-23

The parable of the seed (cf. Third Reading) is a clear reference to the mission of the Church: to spread the Word of God and to help man accept this Word.

The Church opened immediately to the pagan world, generously encouraging others to accept the Good News; what St. Paul did in a few short years is incredible. With Emperor Constantine the persecutions ended and the Church developed the catechumenate to instruct her future members. The instructions were based on the Bible. In the Middle Ages theology was presented in a very systematic way and the Bible remained the basis of the Church's instructions.

In the 16th Century, in response to Protestantism, the Church presented her teachings in concise articles giving more importance to her teaching authority. Under the influence of Illuminism in the 18th and 19th centuries, the Church returned to the Bible. Vatican II not only encourages everyone to read the Bible (cf. Dogmatic Constitution on Divine Revelation, nos. 22 and 24), but insists that the Word of God be the basis of the Church's teaching (cf. Constitution on the Sacred Liturgy, no. 35).

Why does the Church continue, day after day, to sow the Word of God? In the history of salvation, the Word of God is the means of communication (cf. 1 Corinthians 1:21) between God and man. For the non-believer, the Word of God is an invitation or a charism; for those about to be baptized, it is their instruction; and for the practicing Christian, the Word of God is a source of reflection and strength. The Church defends and disseminates the Word of God, because it is this Word which renders the Church one, holy, catholic and apostolic. One, because it is this Word of God that distinguishes it from the pagans. Holy, because the Word is the seed of sanctity. Catholic, because this Word transcends all languages and satisfies man's needs. And apostolic, because the Church has spread this Good News throughout the world and still does so. The Church lives and flourishes today in spite of all the attempts to destroy it, precisely because she possesses "grace and truth" (cf. John 1:14).

The everlasting struggle between light and darkness goes on today as always. Many consider as morally acceptable that untruth, that if it helps a person achieve his purpose, it is fine. It is not difficult to manipulate the facts. Pope Pius XII once said: "Our era is an era of untruth."

If we want to find the truth, we must accept the invitation of Isaiah the prophet: "Let the wicked forsake his way, and the unrighteous man his thoughts; let him return to the Lord that he may have mercy on him" (Isaiah 55:7). In order to live and enjoy the truth, we must receive the Word of God (cf. Second Reading). If we ask God, He will open our hearts to accept His Word (cf. Acts 16:14).

PASTORAL REFLECTIONS

1. *The Christian grows strong nourished by the Word of God.* Modern day mass media immerses us in an ocean of words where truth is not always important. Compromises, lack of sincerity, and importance given to material things render the Christian's life difficult. He will be able to conquer the world (cf. 1 John 5:4) if he knows how to appreciate the Word of God.

2. *Our sanctity is related to the Word of God.* John the apostle tells us that sanctity is the fruit of light (cf. John 8:12). The divine Word is "like a hammer, shattering rocks" (cf. Jeremiah 23:29), like a "two-edged sword" (cf. Hebrews 4:12). The Gospels are "the power of God" (cf. Romans 1:16) which always produce an effect (cf. Isaiah 55:10). The Gospels are "spirit and life" (cf. John 6:63), "justice" (cf. John 12:48), "joy and happiness of heart" (cf. Jeremiah 15:16); they are "our salvation" (cf. John 8:31-47). This is why "we must put the theology of Revelation before the theology of liberation" (Paul VI, April 27, 1975). The world hungers and thirsts for the truth (cf. Amos 8:11-13).

3. *The Christian always accepts this truth.* Here on earth our goal is to listen to this divine Word which makes us friends and followers of Christ (cf. John 15:15). In heaven we will be happy because we see God as He is (cf. John 3:2); on earth our peace and happiness is proportioned to our acceptance of the Gospels. "Listen, children of light. Listen, my dear ones, and rejoice in the Lord. Listen to what you already know, remember

what you have heard. Love what you believe, and preach what you love: Christ is the Truth, Christ is the Light!" (an ancient liturgical hymn)

SIXTEENTH SUNDAY IN ORDINARY TIME

Catechism for Children

Readings: Wisdom 12:13, 16-19
Romans 8:26-27
Matthew 13:24-43

The Word of God is efficient, but it needs someone to disseminate it. Today's liturgy is an excellent lesson in pastoral methodology (cf. Third Reading).

In order to reveal the Good News to children, it is necessary to know them well. Childhood is the time of sense interest, of wonder and candor. Curiosity animates the child; he has an abundance of energy and enthusiasm, always ready for adventure. Children easily identify with and imitate their heroes. Children spontaneously contemplate beauty, truth and goodness. The child naturally tends towards God.

Children have a right and a need to dialogue with God. The goal of evangelization is to lead man to God through Christ. The passage from natural reality to divine reality is personal; it is not the fruit of culture or education. The child can find his responsibility and capacity to love in Christ. How can children be led to Christ? First of all, it is necessary to accept the child for what he is, be ready to walk with him, adapt ourselves to his world. St. Paul was a master in adapting himself to others. With the Hebrews he began with the Old Testament (cf. Acts 13:15-41). With the simple people like the Galatians he began with historical events (cf. Galatians 3:1). For the doctors in Athens, he began with natural theology and cosmic religion (cf. Acts 17:22-31). Every child has a family and social background; the more we know about these, the easier it will be to understand the child.

Children must be loved unconditionally (cf. First Reading). Children should be loved simply because they are children; they should not have to learn or merit love. If our love for a child is sincere and disinterested, the effects will be lasting.

Once we have established a sincere friendship with a child it is possible to help him live and grow in virtue. It is useless to dictate pre-established norms to the child and even worse to bribe him. Virtue is in the child; we should help him to discover and realize it.

Children enjoy listening to the marvelous story of our salvation, indeed a story of love and adventure. It is not necessary to go into many details and explanations; to grasp one truth is, in a certain sense, to grasp all truth. Patiently and lovingly repeat the same truth until the child is able to grasp it.

The prophet Jonah preached penance for forty days before Nineveh repented. To help us remember the divinity of Christ, the Church repeats frequently in the liturgy: "Through Jesus Christ our Lord, God, who lives and reigns forever." As the child grows physically, his capacity to grasp more of the truth increases.

Children want to see. They have a vivid and active imagination. Children express much emotion over small things. A Chinese proverb expresses it in this way: "Children find everything in an apparent nothing; adults find nothing in everything." It is important to help the child to live his emotions in a positive way and fix them as part of his everyday life.

We must not overlook the values of modern mass media. There is a religious application in every aspect of the child's reality: his family, his society, his play. Everything has its place and importance along the way which leads to God.

Children need movement. Psychologists teach us that children learn easier in an atmosphere of play. Children who play well are those who later work well. Teamwork comes naturally to children. They enjoy competition. They never tire of discovering new truths.

The child has a great need to experiment what he has been able to understand; the learning process is something personal.

PASTORAL REFLECTIONS

1. Those who teach children should have the necessary requisites. *The first requisite is human balance.* A person who has problems maintaining order should not attempt to teach catechism. The person who has doubts about what he is teaching should first resolve his doubts; otherwise, he will spread his doubts rather than communicate conviction.

2. *The catechist must have the Word of God in him,* in its threefold form: Scripture, Tradition and the teaching of the Church. "The one who speaks is to deliver God's message" (cf. 1 Peter 4:11). In order to become messengers of God's Word, we must first absorb this Word. The Apostles first believed; and then urged by faith, they spoke (cf. 1 Thessalonians 4:14-15).

3. In supernatural logic, *suffering is apostolic fertility.* "In order to have an impact on all men and to contribute to the salvation of the whole world, much tribulation is necessary" (Decree on the Apostolate of the Laity, no. 16). Frequently the catechist's suffering is reduced to patience, waiting for the fruits of his teaching rather than seeking pedagogical results. The catechist will be misunderstood and criticized and at times he will feel alone; these are the sufferings which verify the true apostle.

SEVENTEENTH SUNDAY IN ORDINARY TIME

The Covenant and God's Love

Readings: 1 Kings 3:5, 7-12
Romans 8:28-30
Matthew 13:44-52

In the Second Reading of today's liturgy St. Paul has synthesized the history of our covenant with God in the following four points: 1) man's creation with the possibility of dialogue with God; 2) man's elevation to the covenant; 3) man's opposition to this elevation, that is, sin; 4) the new promise realized by the future Redeemer.

From a human point of view this plan is not too coherent, but the explanation is simple: God's infinite love. This love gives a salvific dimension to all the events of man's history.

The entire Bible is a story of divine love. As soon as man rebelled, God promised salvation. God called Abraham to the covenant. God confided His secrets to Abraham and he, drawn by love, left his homeland (cf. Second Reading). He was questioned and examined about the essence of God and His love. Abraham was then put to a test when God invited him to sacrifice his son. Moses, from the moment God called him to save His people, grew in knowledge of God and His longing to be man's friend. The prophets Isaiah, Hosea, Jeremiah and Ezekiel were inspired to describe the drama of this divine love; in some instances it almost seems to be jealousy. The Book of Deuteronomy, the Psalms and Ezekiel present God's love as a relationship with the individual; God does not love collectively but singly. In spite of our trials, sufferings and hardships we are invited not to doubt this love.

God's love reached its maximum manifestation when He gave Christ to man. In Christ we can see the infinity of divine charity; in no way did man merit this abundance of love. Christ's life and death and His teachings are the "Good News" of divine love. The Gospels and the letters of the Apostles are the documentation of His love.

PASTORAL REFLECTIONS

1. *God loves us.* "All the bells of the world are not sufficient to remind us of our good fortune: God loves us! The Incarnation and Redemption through Christ are

God's economy of love; this is what Christianity is all about. Christianity is all that takes place within the orbit of God's infinite love for us. Man's dignity and the sacredness of human life come from the fact that God loves us, He loves all men. How then can we segregate men, hate others and do harm to those God loves? In this context we can understand the life of the Apostles, the missionaries and the pastoral life of the Church. Why should I love others? Because God loves them" (Paul VI, February 16, 1977).

2. *The basic alternative of our life is:* either to accept and grow in God's love or refuse it and be spiritually dead (cf. John 3:36). Only he who accepts to be invaded by divine Love is a Christian. St. Augustine said: "I leave my past to the mercy of God, the present to His love and the future to His providence" (cf. Second Reading).

3. *An act of consecration to the infinite love of God:* "Infinite Love, eternal God, principal and source of life, I give myself to You with all my will, take possession of me. I am nothing, incapable of serving You, yet You gave me life and You desire me. Here I am, ready for Your love, ready to make You known throughout the entire world, inasmuch as this is possible for me. I want to do Your will at any cost; I am even ready to shed my blood for You in the hope that it is worthy of Your glory" (Margheret Luisa de La Touche).

EIGHTEENTH SUNDAY IN ORDINARY TIME

Hunger in the World

Readings: Isaiah 55:1-3
Romans 8:35, 37-39
Matthew 14:13-21

The multiplication of the five loaves of bread to feed some ten thousand people brings to light the striking contrast between divine Providence and starvation.

The statistics dealing with hunger are frightening. Perhaps nobody really knows just how many hungry people there are in the world today, or how many children die each day simply because they are undernourished. We do not know how many people do not develop physically and mentally because they do not have a proper diet (cf. Paul VI, *Populorum progressio*, no. 45). It is true that many factors have contributed to this situation. The causes are recent and remote, personal and collective, social and political, natural and egoistic. It is useful to have clear ideas about these causes; let us take a look at some of them.

1. Frequently the events of nature, which is abused by man, destroy crops; such phenomena as drought, hurricanes, and floods destroy enormous amounts of food.

2. There is no doubt that the world population is increasing; each year there are about eighty million more mouths to feed. Thanks to science, today people live longer.

3. It is not something rare to read about the destruction of tons of fruit or vegetables or rivers of milk to maintain prices which are threatened by overproduction.

4. There is another curious fact in the world today. It appears that some countries prefer not to cultivate their abundant and fertile soil but to develop the war industry. They import much of their foodstuffs in exchange for war machinery and frequently those who produce the food need it more than the war machinery.

5. The commercial profits of the war industry are incredible. Something has gone wrong somewhere in the heart of man when he spends billions of dollars per year for arms.

6. Fertilizers cost more because petroleum costs more. Agricultural machinery is insufficient where it is most needed.

7. Technical cooperation in agriculture on an international level is sadly lacking. Agrarian economies are

frequently subordinated to techniques and profits; consequently, many people have lost an interest in their land.

8. At times man's tendency to hoard makes food more scarce for those who need it.

The problem is serious and there is no easy solution. In the next twenty-five years the demographic growth will continue and to what extent the so-called "green revolution" will be effective is not known. But this does not mean that starvation and undernourishment are the inevitable fates of the less fortunate; things can be redimensioned if everyone gets involved. "We must not panic nor get discouraged; rather, the urgency and priority of this problem should urge us to find a solution. The time has come to admit that our organizations have gone astray and to take the necessary remedies" (Paul VI, Message to the F.A.O., November 9, 1974).

We can make numerous efforts to have a modern day "miracle of the multiplication of the loaves."

1. The developing countries need assistance both through monetary funds to develop agriculture and an exchange of technicians and technical know-how.

2. The food and grain reserves should be accessible to all nations with as little red tape as possible.

3. Agriculture is not a feudal system that can be abused by those who are strong. Those who have everything they need also have a responsibility towards those who are in need. Human solidarity should be free of any speculation or political pride. Investments should be in peace, not in war; in human solidarity, not in an egoistic economy. Social justice is more than simply "do not steal," it is also "know how to share."

4. Abundance is a gift of God; we should not waste our riches. Consumption should be a means, not an end. We must learn how to follow the instruction of Jesus: "Gather up the fragments left over, that nothing may be lost" (John 6:12). If we can overcome the temptation of abundance, there will be more for others.

5. Considering the fact that only about sixteen percent of the usable soil is actually being cultivated, it would seem logical to cultivate more.

6. No one knows the potential of nature; there is much in nature which has yet to be discovered and explored for the benefit of man (cf. Paul VI, November 9, 1974 and November 10, 1974).

7. Those who work the soil should do so with dedication and technical organization. "It is necessary that the farmer be faithful to his profession and at the same time make every effort to increase his culture in order to free agriculture" (Paul VI, November 9, 1974).

8. It is evident that some sort of change is necessary. The key to the success of any change is man's heart. In our era of superactivity there are frequent changes and transformations on all levels. Perhaps in our frenetic activity we fail to see that no technical or organizational change can be efficient unless man's spirit is also modified. "A good law is useless if it is for people with an evil spirit; a mediocre law is valid and useful when man has good intentions" (Montesquieu).

PASTORAL REFLECTIONS

1. *The Church has taken an active interest in the problem of hunger.* Just to mention some of the more official documents we can recall: *Rerum novarum* of Leo XIII, *Quadragesimo anno* of Pius XI, *Pacem in terris* of John XXIII, the *Pastoral Constitution on the Church in the Modern World* of Vatican II, *Populorum progressio* and *Octogesima adveniens* of Paul VI. Pope Paul's two messages to the F.A.O. in November of 1974 are an excellent example of the Church's interest in eliminating hunger in the world. The spirit of the Church's message has always been to animate work with charity and to animate our personal sanctity with love of our fellow man.

2. *The Christian must make every effort to free the world of its material evils.* The Christian has a double

citizenship: spiritual citizen of the Church and temporal citizen of this world. The two must be integrated. "Religious convictions are not like candles which are put out once the celebration is over; they are a light which remains in our conscience and guides our activity. Our Christian life must be coherent" (Paul VI, January 2, 1977).

3. The Church must be involved in the things of the world in the reality of this earth, and, consequently, needs a certain *structural organization.* Those who wish to do away with the visible Church ignore the authentic reality of the ecclesial life.

NINETEENTH SUNDAY IN ORDINARY TIME

The Theology of Crisis in the Church

Readings: 1 Kings 19:9, 11-13
Romans 9:1-5
Matthew 14:22-33

Even when we are near Jesus we can be tried. The Church can be in crisis and this "causes great pain and constant suffering" (cf. Second Reading and Third Reading).

It is natural to ask: why?

1. The crises and trials are an essential element of the double life of the Church. St. Augustine wrote: "The Church has a double life. The one is lived in faith, the other in vision; the one in time and struggles, the other in rest in the eternal homeland. One is lived in action, the other in the reward of the Vision; one flees from evil, the other does good. One contends with the enemy, the other has no enemy; one fights the desires of the flesh, the other is spiritual joy. One is battle weary, the other enjoys the peace of victory. One seeks and obtains pardon, the other has nothing to forgive. One is tormented by evil in order to remain humble in the good received,

the other is free of every evil and participates in the Supreme Good. The first is represented by Peter, the second by John" (St. Augustine: Commentary on the Gospel of St. John, 124-5). "To convince His followers that He had really risen, Christ kept the signs of the crucifixion; likewise He is wounded in His Church so that we can believe in His presence and resurrection" (St. Leo the Great, Homily, 74). We could add another sign to the traditional four: One, Holy, Catholic, Apostolic and Persecuted.

2. Vatican Council II clearly indicates the intention of the Church to be inserted in the earthly reality. This is not easy, and the Church is still struggling to find the best way to realize this intention. Part of the Church's crisis is due to this "breaking in" period.

3. There seems to be a great distance between modern thought and religious mentality. Modern education is anthropocentric, while religion is theocentric (cf. Paul VI, February 9, 1972). The treasures of wisdom and goodness which seemed to be a patrimony of the Church are absorbed by other cultures to the point where the Church loses her purpose to exist (cf. Paul VI, September 11, 1974).

4. Another reason for crisis in the Church is materialism and hedonism and other ways to approve sin, but Christ said: "He who is in sin detests the light."

5. There are Christians who attack the Church in the name of "fidelity to the gospels." Some abandon the Church saying that it is basically corrupt. Others give the Church a secondary function to their charisms and prophetic vocations. More dangerous are those who externally remain faithful but intend to change the Church as if the Church must begin with them.

6. New experiences and original ideas have a certain attraction; novelty becomes, as it were, a criterion of truth and authenticity. In this context, it is a short step to want to eliminate Tradition.

7. Much criticism of the Church is not well reasoned. When emotions substitute reason, there is a danger of

confusing an abundance of words with the truth. Where reasoning decreases, atheism increases. In the Middle Ages the Christian was led almost exclusively by faith, which was not an ideal situation, but today there seems to be a tendency to substitute faith with sentiments which generate confusion and crises for Christians.

This list of causes could go on and on, but perhaps it is more profitable to think about a remedy.

There is no need to be discouraged; God has promised "that we should be saved from our enemies, and from the hand of all who hate us" (Luke 1:71). God uses human defeat to bring about His victory; heavenly light coincides with earthly darkness. Every defeat is followed by brilliant revival.

It is the eternal drama of Good Friday which prepares for the resurrection. "The resurrection is a school of strength and hope. It teaches us that the trials of life can give rise to unexpected comfort" (Paul VI, March 6, 1977).

The history of the Church confirms this. The heresies of the first centuries gave birth to the Dogmatic Councils of Nicea (325), Constantinople (381), Ephesus (431) and Chalcedon (451). St. Augustine said: "There were many heresies so that we would not remain infants."

With the barbarian invasions of the fifth century, it seemed that Christianity was doomed. Instead it was the barbarians who defended and spread the teaching of Christ.

In the tenth century the Church suffered a crisis of authority, which was eventually solved by Pope Gregory VII.

With time the crises became more frequent, there was secularization, naturalism, new discoveries, and other such causes. Each crisis was met with new life in the Church. This was the period of the origin of many great religious orders.

In the sixteenth century many were led from Rome by Luther, Calvin, Zwingli and Henry VIII. This period also produced the Council of Trent and numerous saints.

In the last century the Church withstood the crisis of illuminism and in our times there is materialism and positivism. It is possible to injure the Church but not eliminate her.

The Church is offended and yet offers pardon, is denied and is patient, is trampled upon and always rises. It must be so as Christ promised: "I am with you always, until the end of the ages" (Matthew 28:20).

PASTORAL REFLECTIONS

1. Passing from the theoretical and historical to the practical, *it is necessary to exercise our faith*. When the prophet Habakkuk witnessed the apparent ruin of the chosen people, he complained to God about it. God led him to understand that it was to increase his faith; he then uttered his famous words: "The just man, because of his faith, shall live" (Habakkuk 2:4). "Faith is the first condition to overcome difficulty. St. John the apostle said our faith is the victory which conquers the world" (Paul VI, September 11, 1974).

2. *Faith generates hope.* The present crisis seems perhaps worse than any of the past. This is a call for hope. Christ has strengthened the Church with the Holy Spirit, a sure guarantee of victory in any crisis. "The Church has her revenge and victory on those who persecute her. The revenge is to pray for them, the victory is to outlive them" (Charles Montalembert).

Father Charles de Foucauld was put to death in the Sahara desert in 1916. Before his death he said: "Don't be surprised by this storm. The ship of Peter has withstood others even more violent. Think of what the small community in Rome went through when Peter and Paul were put to death. They were not discouraged; they are an example of hope."

3. *We must love the Church* simply because the Church is marvelous. The Church is perfect in essence, even if inperfect in her external manifestations. St. Augustine said it is an error to leave the Church for some technical mistake without considering all the good the Church continues to do for the glory of Christ.

The Church is a mother. Mothers cry, mothers suffer, mothers forgive, mothers hope and mothers love. If one has all the reasons in the world not to love his mother, he is always outside of love.

TWENTIETH SUNDAY IN ORDINARY TIME

The Universality of the Church

Readings: Isaiah 56:1, 6-7
Romans 11:13-15, 29-32
Matthew 15:21-28

If the Church is trampled on by some, it is simply to enable her to offer God's mercy to others. The Church is a pilgrim throughout the world, sensitizing humanity to reconcile with God.

The call of Abraham to be the father of a great people is a prefiguration of the universality of the Church (cf. Genesis 12). More than the others, Isaiah the prophet foresees the universality of God's kingdom (cf. Isaiah 49:6, 52:10).

Christ spent most of His time with the Hebrew people. However, He said salvation was also for others. So He did dialogue with others: the Samaritan woman, the centurion and the Canaanite woman (cf. Third Reading).

Peter was the first to open the doors of the Church to non-believers. He wanted to free religion from its bondage to Mosaic law (cf. 2 Peter 3:9). Direct conversion to Christ without a certain historical background is perfectly legitimate (cf. Acts 2:1-18). The champion of the universality of the Church was Paul. He was in contact with three civilizations: born in the Greek city of Tarsus, of Jewish parents, he was a Roman citizen. He knew the Greek culture, had studied the Scriptures and the Laws, and had free access to the Roman Empire. Christ made him the Apostle of the Gentiles (cf. Acts 9:15). He was the universal Apostle. In his journeys and in his writings his ideal is clear: "For though I am free from all men, I have made myself a slave to all, that I might win the more. To the Jews I became as a Jew, in order to win Jews; to those under the law I became as one under the law that I might win those under the law. To those outside the law I became as one outside the law that I might win those outside the law. To the weak I became weak, that I might win the weak. I have become all things to all men that I might by all means save some" (1 Corinthians 9:19-23). His sole interest was the salvation of as many as possible (cf. 1 Corinthians 10:33).

All the early Fathers, in one way or another, spoke of the universality of the Church. St. Ignatius of Antioch was the first to use the word "catholic." Writing to the faithful of Smyrna he said: "Where Christ is, there is the Catholic Church."

What exactly do we mean when we say the Church is Catholic? All creation and all history is related to the Church, and this is sufficient to explain the entire world. Rather than simply the visible or universal kingdom of God, the Church is the Sacrament of history. The Good News of Christ must reach everyone; only then will history be complete. The Jewish people who have separated from the Church have not been abandoned; it is possible for them to accept the Messiah (cf. Romans 11:26). It must be possible for all men to accept the invitation of God and thus realize the universality of salvation. The Church has the mission to establish the kingdom of Christ among all people (cf. Dogmatic Constitution on the Church, no. 5). The Church Christ established after His resurrection is just a beginning, which will terminate with the history of mankind.

PASTORAL REFLECTIONS

1. *Every Christian is called to participate in the universality of the Church.* A Christian has not only a prospective future but also an operative future. The Good News of God's kingdom has been proclaimed, and people of every sort are entering (cf. Mark 16:16). Vatican Council II has given a new impetus to the missionary activity of the Church (cf. Decree on the Church's Missionary Activity, nos. 1, 2). In the past, religious orders carried out most of the missionary activity; however, every Christian community has received the mandate to share the Good News with all men without limitation (cf. Paul VI, May 17, 1974).

2. The *pastoral methodology* of the missions must be understood in the proper perspective. The missions are not to be considered as an extension of the central Church; they are part of the very essence of the Church (cf. Decree on the Church's Missionary Activity). Saint John Bosco encouraged his missionaries to carry out a three-point plan. First, work with the emigrants to give them help. Second, make contact with the non-believers, revealing the light of the Word of God. Third, help the local Christian communities grow, and with them the kingdom of Christ will grow.

3. *Universality is a natural consequence of the fullness of truth.* This truth, brought by Christ, is always applicable in any and every historical situation, to any and every ethnic group. The Holy Spirit was given to the Church for this reason (cf. John 16:13). The basic truths of the Church are always the same, the external aspects can and do change. It is not possible to go back to a certain period and stop the dynamic growth of the Church.

TWENTY-FIRST SUNDAY IN ORDINARY TIME

The Church and Peter

Readings: Isaiah 22:15, 19-23
Romans 11:33-36
Matthew 16:13-20

Every organization has its headquarters and someone who is responsible for the organization. The nation has its president, the city its mayor, the business concern its director, and so on. It is logical that Christ wanted to give His Church an authority, a point of reference, an energetic source for the entire Mystical Body. Peter received this primacy, and it has been passed on through the centuries to his successors.

It is evident from the particular attention that Christ gave to Peter that He had something special in mind for this impulsive and generous fisherman. Christ prepared Peter to become the visible leader of His Church.

The most evident proof of this is the clear promise Christ made: "Now when Jesus came into the district of Caesarea Philippi, he asked his disciples, 'Who do men say that the Son of man is?' And they said, 'Some say John the Baptist, others say Elijah, and others Jeremiah or one of the prophets.' He said to them, 'But who do you say that I am?' Simon Peter replied, 'You are the Christ, the Son of the living God.' And Jesus answered him, 'Blessed are you, Simon Bar-Jona! For flesh and blood has not revealed this to you, but my Father who is in heaven. And I tell you, you are Peter, and on this rock I will build my Church, and the powers of death shall not prevail against it. I will give you the keys of the kingdom of heaven, and whatever you bind on earth shall be bound in heaven, and whatever you loose on earth shall be loosed in heaven'" (Matthew 16:13-20).

There are four basic reasons which support the primacy of Peter. The fact that his name was changed: in the biblical mentality to change a person's name means to give him a special task.

Peter is presented as the foundation of the Church, a solid rock foundation which will last in time. Christ's intention was to found a Church, and, consequently, He gave it a solid, lasting foundation (cf. John 2:19; Mark 14:58). God is the rock of refuge (cf. Psalms 31:3; 71:3). Abraham is the basis of the faith in the world; Peter is the foundation of God's Church.

The third reasoning is the symbolism of the keys. In our absence we will give the keys of our home to a friend who will look after it for us. Christ entrusted to Peter the full responsibility of opening or closing the doors of His Church, of opening and closing His Kingdom.

The person who has the power to let others enter or to close the door to them must also have the ability to know who, when and how the others are to enter. The juridical power of the keys is completed by the charismatic and doctrinal power of judgment. The power to "bind and loose" was also given to the other Apostles (cf. Matthew 18:18); however, it was given in a particular and discriminate way to Peter (cf. Matthew 16:19). The Apostles and bishops can use this power for their particular churches, whereas Peter can use it for the universal Church.

The association of Peter with rock indicates the objective doctrinal stability and the subjective decisional strength, while the invitation to feed His sheep reveals the kindness and dedication of the pastor towards the flock (cf. Paul VI, February 10, 1975).

It is easy to understand how the life of the Holy Father is full of suffering. Like Christ, he is a sign of contradiction and must absorb all the reactions to his delicate pastoral activity. Beginning with Peter and up to Sixtus II who died in the year 258 A.D., the first twenty-four Popes were martyred. In a certain sense we can say in every century of the Church's history there has been a persecuted Pope. Even in our present times there have been threats and complaints hurled against the Vicar of Christ.

PASTORAL REFLECTIONS

1. *The papacy is necessary to transmit the light of the truth.* Living things tend to open towards the light. Without the sun, without light, there would be no life. Without the light of truth, there is no supernatural life. Christ instituted the Church so that men would always have the truth. He made Peter the leader, giving him the command to see to it that His sheep are nourished with the truth. "The chair of Peter is the centripetal force of the Christian faith of all the various communities; it radiates this faith to the entire world" (Paul VI, January 3, 1977). Christ allowed Peter the freedom to betray Him, but He did not allow him to lose his faith, as he had to confirm the faith of the others. No matter how deeply humanity is immersed in the darkness of error and untruth, the light of truth shines to direct man, if he so desires, towards his homeland.

2. *The papacy is a blessing for the members of the Church.* The faithful have always considered and appreciated the Pope as the guardian of Christ's teachings. In moments of doubt and uncertainty the early Christians went to Peter to solve their problems and receive encouragement. Pilgrims go to Rome not simply to visit the tombs of Peter and Paul but to hear the teachings and encouragement of Peter's successor. The founders of the various religious societies and congregations have always had great care to act in full harmony with the Pope. It seems rather absurd to want to consider all the various opinions, which can be more or less interesting, and at the same time to exclude *a priori* the voice of the Vicar of Christ.

3. *It takes faith to adhere to the teachings of the Pope.* This is particularly true when these teachings are not in harmony with our limited opinion. It is easy to respect and obey the Holy Father and the bishops when they are benevolent and their teachings agree with our ideas. It requires faith to see things in a more universal way and accept instructions which are not in full agreement with our desires. The main task of Peter's successor is to guide souls, to give them the truth, but not to accommodate them in all the variations of time.

TWENTY-SECOND SUNDAY IN ORDINARY TIME

The Way of the Cross

Readings: Jeremiah 20:7-9
Romans 12:1-2
Matthew 16:21-27

Suffering is a reality. Three aspects of this reality worthy of our reflection are: every man is subject to suffering, how we react to suffering and the utility of suffering.

Happiness seems to be a constant desire, while suffering is a harsh reality. The cross is a tree which can give good and abundant fruit; the Son of God chose it as His throne to give us life and love, as His pulpit to teach us truth.

Suffering helps us to understand our existence; it is part of our life. In order to develop our true personality, it is necessary to learn how to suffer. If we are not able to suffer, we remain infantile. Life comes to be in the suffering of childbirth, and if it is to mature, it will be in suffering. "God has given man the possibility to enjoy many things, but the price is fatigue; on every work of art there are tears" (Leonardo da Vinci). From the non-Christian point of view, pleasure is the goal of life; for the Christian, pleasure is a reward.

If we do not know how to suffer, we cannot understand others, we cannot love; when we know how to accept suffering, we become capable of loving.

Maturity is tied to the mysterious condition of suffering. A mountain climber first crosses the green pastures, then the hills, afterwards the rocky mountain and the sheer slopes, and finally the peak. The weak plants are distinguished from the strong ones when they are buffeted by winds. Adversity and difficulty stimulate thought, motivate the will and purify the heart. Suffering opens the way to genius.

Dante Alighieri lived an extremely difficult life; he was exiled and condemned to death in his absence. The life of Michelangelo was certainly not a life of joy and pleasure. Beethoven was deaf and constantly afflicted with family problems. Giuseppe Verdi created "Nabucco" after the cruel death of his wife and children. Dostoevski had to write in exile.

In a religious and supernatural context, suffering is even more fertile. Suffering purifies us. Frequently our tears become light which enable us to see better. "Suffering improves man" (Ampère). Suffering burns like fire, but cleans like soap. It scratches like sandpaper, but removes rust. It is bitter, but strengthens like medicine. At times we lose sight of our final goal in life; suffering helps us to reorient ourselves. "When a man of good will suffers, in that very moment he realizes he needs God. Without God he can do nothing" *(The Imitation of Christ)*. Frequently, loneliness brings us to God's presence.

Suffering is the way to heaven (cf. John 14:6). Christ entered the glory of His Father through suffering. If we intend to be glorified, we must accept to be crucified (cf. 1 Peter 4:13). The worst punishment is God's silence. In this context we can better understand the Old Testament mentality that God punished His people to bring them closer to Him: "God chastises those He loves." The dynamics of the spiritual life are: from death to life; from suffering to love; from sadness to joy. Suffering can be a sure sign of salvation (cf. Jeremiah 29:10-12).

PASTORAL REFLECTIONS

1. *We cannot live in love without suffering.* Love is caring for the needs of others before our own. Love is being responsible for the one loved; love is respecting the one loved. Love is the ability to give even without receiving; in this context love involves suffering.

2. *Suffering makes us images of Christ.* "The image on a coin is impressed under pressure and heat; the image of a Christian is impressed by the suffering of the Son of God" (St. Ignatius of Antioch). "If we want to reflect the promise of salvation, we must model our lives on Christ crucified" (St. Francis of Assisi). "The Head has suffered; if the members wish to be worthy of their Head they too must suffer" (St. Augustine). "It is a shame when a member does not want to suffer, considering that the Head is covered with thorns" (St. Bernard).

3. *The apostle is one who suffers.* Christ continues the salvation of man through the suffering of His members. Christ prolongs His passion in His followers. The condemnation of Christ was not just a point of arrival for the prophecies; it was also a point of departure to extend the kingdom of God throughout the world. From this Christian point of view suffering makes sense.

TWENTY-THIRD SUNDAY IN ORDINARY TIME

Dialogue and Fraternal Correction

Readings: Ezekiel 33:7-9
Romans 13:8-10
Matthew 18:15-20

Dialogue and fraternal correction are not easy. The following basic considerations can be useful.

1. There are three moments to dialogue: awareness and acceptance of those with different ideas, the confrontation of ideas, and the readiness to change an idea in the light of new elements which might emerge during the conversation. Dialogue means a passage from one aspect of the truth. The word truth means "a reality to be discovered." No one has a monopoly on truth. In its objective nature truth is one, but subjectively each one of us can absorb one or more aspects of it. It is something like a large mosaic, to which we all can contribute several pieces.

2. The basic attitude during dialogue is Christian charity. We must speak with our hearts. It is not a struggle or a contest.

3. There is no room for prejudice. If men were as evil as some indicate, it would be impossible to live. If men were as good as others would have them, life would be stagnant. We can always learn something from others. Christ dialogued with everyone: children and adults, honest people and sinners, learned and illiterate, friends and enemies, rich and poor, men and women, those in authority and the man in the street.

4. To know how to listen is very useful. Before speaking it is important to think about what must be said, how and when to say it and why the truth is sought. When speaking, keep calm. Say the proper thing at the proper time. It is not necessary to be always talking; there are moments when listening in silence is more opportune.

5. We must overcome the temptation to play on the meaning of words or to separate their meaning from our lives. St. Paul tells us that the new man is clothed in "sincerity and truth" (cf. 1 Corinthians 5:8). This truth has three dimensions: a relationship with God, a relationship with ourselves, and a relationship with others.

6. Christ is the fullness of truth. Leaving Christ out means groping in the dark. He is the light; He is the personification of truth. When Christians intend to solve religious problems, they must refer to the words of Christ, and they should not exclude the words of His Vicar on earth.

7. Faith must be the basis of every dialogue (cf. First Reading). The purpose of Revelation is to enlighten and guide all men; consequently, its substance does not change. There can be dialogue concerning the pastoral application of faith, but not about the content of faith.

8. Dialogue based on faith has as its final goal our salvation. Whenever God speaks, He does so as our Savior. The ideal or intention of Christian dialogue should be salvation. To possess the truth in biblical language means to be along the way to salvation. Outside this perspective there can be no dialogue in the full Christian sense.

9. In relation to salvation it is necessary to speak the truth clearly and completely as it is revealed in the Scriptures (cf. First Reading). "You are able to give advice to one another" (Romans 15:14). The prophets always spoke boldly and with certainty, kind towards those who were in error but firm in denouncing the error. "We must say no to all forms of evil" (John XXIII, August 29, 1959). It might be convenient at times not to reveal the truth, but this is an omission and not pleasing to God (cf. Isaiah 56:10). To stop the spread of evil we must speak the truth even if it is not pleasant. One of the basic elements of friendship is to be able to speak the truth freely at all times.

10. When all attempts at dialogue fail, the Gospels suggest (cf. Third Reading) to refer the matter to the

assembly. If we consider that someone might be risking his eternal salvation, this is not a drastic action. Before acting in this manner, however, we must be living witnesses of the truth.

PASTORAL REFLECTIONS

1. *In order to dialogue well we must be in the presence of Christ.* When Thomas doubted Christ's resurrection, Jesus was not present. Later when Christ appeared and Thomas was present, he behaved differently (cf. John 20:24-29).

2. *When we dialogue in the name of Christ, our dialogue can become prayer.* "For where two or three are gathered in my name, there I am in the midst of them" (Matthew 18:20). How wonderful it would be if every meeting could be a Eucharistic Celebration.

3. *A proposal for our lives:* "Man has lived side by side with his fellowmen far too long. Today it is necessary to live together; we must learn to live for the others. The only truth is to love one another" (Follereau).

TWENTY-FOURTH SUNDAY IN ORDINARY TIME

Violence and Pardon

Readings: Sirach 27:30—28:7
Romans 14:7-9
Matthew 18:21-35

Physical violence and double standards are part of the society we live in. There are various reasons for this sad situation; today's liturgy gives us the possibility to consider two of these causes.

The official in the parable evidently had serious problems in organizing his life as he had an enormous debt. This points more to a way of life than to an emergency situation. In all probability he wanted to live without working. Idleness is conducive to vice and violence.

The official became furious with the servant simply because he had one ideal in life: money. He was unable to see the servant as the head of a family who no doubt had good reasons for his petty debt; all he saw was money. If we stop to consider much of the violence in the world today, it is not difficult to see its relation to money. The materialistic outlook on life renders man nervous and capable of violence, because it excludes man's infinite dimension. When this dimension is missing, man becomes a wolf. In this sense materialism contains the dialect of struggle and violence.

What is the proper Christian attitude in relation to this thorny problem? Christ's answer is pardon.

Peter had been entrusted with the authority to "bind or loose." He had the duty to correct his brothers (cf. Matthew 18:15-18); he wanted some criterion for forgiving those who offended the community. He generously established seven as the maximum, but Christ put no limit. Forgiveness must not be guided by man's finite generosity but by God's infinite generosity.

The theory is beautiful and at the same time extremely difficult, almost contrary to human nature. In practice, there are problems and objections.

The person who has offended others, who has been violent, will take advantage of the situation. The Christian, as an individual, is called to forgive, but this does not impede justice on a social level. The individual is invited to forgive, because "Vengeance is mine, says the Lord" (Romans 12:19). Our religion is a religion of mercy. True forgiveness is a means to help or cure the offender; it can lead him to conversion (cf. Romans 12:20). To forgive means to make a friend of an enemy. Those who are violent and do evil are frequently miserable, and a bit of kindness might change their lives. The satisfaction of love surpasses all the victories of vengeance.

Speaking to a group of pilgrims, who had suffered much violence during the last world war, the Holy Father said: "I admire you, because you have changed hatred into love, revenge into friendship, war into peace. This is true Christianity" (Paul VI, April 4, 1964). "To exchange evil with good is a source of pleasure" (Gandhi).

Another problem in the art of forgiving is the reaction of him who forgives. Knowledge and acceptance of Christ's directive to forgive our enemies does not always eliminate our reactions towards the offender. Christian pardon is an ideal; ideals are never totally achieved; we must constantly strive for them. The ability to forgive is a process of becoming mature, of becoming more like Christ. The first step in this process is to refuse to hate or hold a grudge. The second is not to repay evil with evil. The third step is to be able to speak with the offender. Denounce the evil done, but do not judge the offender, that is, remain neutral towards the offender in society even if we remember the offense. The next step is to be able to take the initiative and be sincerely kind towards the offender. Still another step in this difficult process is the ability to understand and prefer the person who has done us harm. Perfect forgiveness is the ability to love those who harm us in the same way God loves them.

PASTORAL REFLECTIONS

1. We all make mistakes from time to time. Even if we feel we are pretty good, there are things for which *we can ask pardon*. St. Augustine, before his death, said: "If at times I did not receive all those who sought me, if I received you giving the impression of being bored, if at times I spoke harshly, if I failed to help the needy and the afflicted, I beg all of you who suffered because of my shortcomings to forgive me and I assure you that God will forgive you in turn."

2. Forgiveness is a guarantee of eternal life. The violent official was punished because he did not want to forgive the servant (cf. Third Reading). The Arabs say

there are two doors which pass through the Valley of Judgment: one is penance, and the other is mercy and forgiveness. "Above all hold unfailing your love for one another, since love covers a multitude of sins" (1 Peter 4:8). Christ's words are very clear: "If you forgive men their trespasses, your heavenly Father also will forgive you" (Matthew 6:14).

3. The most noble act man is capable of is Christian forgiveness. If we are capable of doing many things but we do not forgive, our activities are of little value. If we have few talents and know how to forgive, our lives will be rich. Forgiveness is the perfection of charity.

TWENTY-FIFTH SUNDAY IN ORDINARY TIME

The Call of God and Love

Readings: Isaiah 55:6-9
Philippians 1:20-24, 27
Matthew 20:1-16

The parable of the laborers in the vineyard is rich in meaning (cf. Third Reading).

The vineyard signifies God's love and care for man. The various moments when the owner hired his workers are God's attempts to establish an eternal covenant with the Jewish people in time: from Adam to Noah, from Noah to Abraham, from Abraham to the Prophets and on to John the Baptist and finally God's Son. It can also be the universality of God's call: first to the Jewish people, then to the pagans of Rome and Greece, followed by the barbarians of Europe and Asia, and finally the invitation to the entire world to embrace and accept Christ's Good News.

On an individual level, God calls us frequently. In our childhood, He calls us through our sentiments; in youth, through our enthusiasm for life; as adults, through our actions; and in our twilight years, through our longing to rest in the Lord.

Why did all the laborers receive the same reward? Those who began at dawn worked more than those who entered the vineyard in the afternoon. To be idle, to be unemployed is not something pleasant; to have work is already a source of security and satisfaction. Socially and psychologically all the laborers had the same needs. Once my rights have been respected, I should rejoice to see others treated with generosity. From an apostolic point of view, as St. John Eudes would say, we are all "useless servants"; in this sense it is absurd to pretend anything.

God does not depend on man. If He intends to be more generous with some rather than with others, He does not have to justify His actions before men (cf. First Reading). These considerations should not lead us to be less generous, thinking that in the end we will all be the same. Considering our eternal reward, we know that everyone will be fully rewarded; however, there can be differences in the ability to receive. The Little Flower expressed this idea well when she said the thimble, the glass and the vase are all perfectly full, yet each has a different value. God will reward everyone with the infinite riches of His love which is qualitatively perfect and indivisible; however, the way in which it is received depends on the ontological and functional ability of each individual.

God's love for man is as old as humanity, since man's creation God has always loved man. God has always made every effort to maintain friendship with man, "having at heart the happiness of man's soul" (cf. St. John Chrysostom). "When man thinks God is unjust he commits the greatest injustice possible against the Infinite Goodness" (Anthony Rosmini).

PASTORAL REFLECTIONS

1. Our reactions depend mostly on our *greed for earthly reality*. The Christian outlook is to seek only what is necessary. Shakespeare was of this same opinion: "If each man would be satisfied with what is conve-

nient, how happy we all would be." We have what we want when we desire what we have. Happiness is being satisfied with our condition and at the same time wanting to improve it, to obtain greater benefit from our life; the desire to have a certain tranquillity with the maximum trust in God.

2. *Those who have consecrated themselves to God* choose to stay with Him at all times, and this is the source of their happiness. "You are happy because you have chosen the better part; because you have given your life to the greatest love. You are the preferred members of the Church, because you participate in the joy and sorrow, fatigue and hope of the Church. Everything you do is rewarded by our Father who reads the hearts of men. Like Mary, you have heard the Word of God and you have accepted it with open arms" (Paul VI, September 11, 1965 and June 29, 1971). St. Columban once asked one of his disciples why he was always happy even when his work was criticized while that of others was praised. The reply was: "Nothing can take from me my God."

3. *The mercy of God is our salvation.* If at times, because of our human weakness, like the prodigal son, we might wander from our Father's house, He is always ready to receive us. "But you, beloved, build yourselves up in your most holy faith; pray in the Holy Spirit; keep yourselves in love of God; wait for the mercy of our Lord Jesus Christ unto eternal life" (Jude 1:20-22).

TWENTY-SIXTH SUNDAY IN ORDINARY TIME

Virtue and Civilization

Readings: Ezekiel 18:25-28
Philippians 2:1-11
Matthew 21:28-32

Social good or evil does not depend so much on the society itself; it depends more on individual responsibility (cf. First Reading).

The history of civilization is the history of man, man considered as body and soul. When man is depressed in spirit, his human-social life is reduced. Present day society, perhaps more so than ever before, wants to get rid of God and fails to see that this is collective suicide. The Church has the solution and can once again help society find its proper orientation. "Many aspects of our society—such as, our knowledge and dominance of nature, our theories of human rights and justice, our notions of world solidarity and assistance to those in need—things which did not exist in earlier times—have been fostered and encouraged by the Gospel" (Vincent Gioberti). Respect for life and death, the equality of men, the notion of freedom and personal responsibility and love of the truth are all Christian principles. The Church has taught and always encouraged honesty rather than utility, benevolence rather than hate, trust and love rather than egoism, human justice rather than the triumph of fleeting ideals. All these human-social values have their origin in the teachings of Christ. It would be both lengthy and boring to illustrate how each of these values originated and developed. It is sufficient to indicate that the great synthesis in the various fields of human knowledge was inspired by the Gospels: literature—*The Divine Comedy*; architecture—the Gothic style; nature—St. Francis; philosophy and theology—Sts. Thomas and Bonaventure. If we were to make a list of the great scientists we would get the impression that the "genius" is part of the Church. The first libraries were the ancient monasteries; the first universities were founded by the Popes.

The influence of the values of the Gospels is also evident in the various civil codes. The Constitution of the United States of America is almost a verbatim copy of St. Robert Bellarmine's treatise on justice which develops four basic points: 1) all men are creatures of God, 2) all men are equal, 3) all men are free and can amend their ways, and 4) it is possible to overcome evil with good. Civilization is conditioned by the spiritual element. "Man's creativity depends on his religious sense" (Johann Wolfgang Von Goethe).

PASTORAL REFLECTIONS

1. An *idea of God is essential for civilization.* An old Russian proverb states: "We can live without a father, we can live without a mother, but we cannot live without God." Over the entrance to the University of Cairo there is this inscription: "Chemistry is necessary but not more important than God." Man is capable of doing something worthwhile, something that will withstand the test of time, only when he operates in the friendship of God. If we lose sight of God everything becomes difficult and personal and social values go to pieces. God is the principle and end of every reality. St. Augustine said: "God is present in every reality." Without God, our activities lack unity; without God, man, life and our nation do not make sense.

2. *The saints have all contributed to the good of society.* Every civilization is closely related to the moral virtues of its members. Ezekiel the prophet teaches us that the presence of good and evil in society depends on the moral attitude of members of the society. The battles and victories of society are not fought and won in government and administration; they depend on the behavior of every individual (cf. First Reading). Science can give us physical power, which will lead to destruction if it is not controlled by man's spiritual power.

The saint gives society that necessary spiritual element. Sanctity unites man to God and to his fellowmen. Sanctity is being like Christ who is God made man.

3. *True civilization includes the transcendental.* History usually categorizes men into those who win and those who lose, those who have and those who do not have. But our life is more than cars, vacations, conventions and politics. There is a spiritual element in man; he

needs goodness, fraternity, hope, enthusiasm. Without this divine element, man's life is without purpose; virtue and moral perfection are essential.

TWENTY-SEVENTH SUNDAY IN ORDINARY TIME

Christian Humanism

Readings: Isaiah 5:1-7
Philippians 4:6-9
Matthew 21:33-43

There are two types of humanism. The first is earthly humanism which has various modifications: intellectual humanism, that is, man can be elevated only by cultural ideas; operative humanism, that is, what is pragmatic is useful; scientific humanism, that is, science and theory are absolute values; materialistic humanism, that is, economic factors are important. These variations are the "spirit of the century." They consider only the horizontal dimension of man. They proclaim man as his own absolute cause. They free man and replace every other obligation. Carried to the extreme man becomes a superbeing (Nietzsche) and God is eliminated (cf. Paul VI, Dec. 25, 1973).

The second type of humanism is Christian humanism, which unites the divine element with earthly reality, which in turn becomes involved in elevating man. This is what St. Paul had in mind when he wrote: "Whatever is true, whatever is honorable, whatever is just, whatever is pure, whatever is lovely, whatever is gracious, if there is any excellence, if there is anything worthy of praise, think about these things" (cf. Second Reading).

This is perhaps the only way to consider the world and justify its riches. In fact, without the idea and the influence of God, the source of life, the universe is meaningless. Without God, reality loses its proportion, and that which man has made absolute works against man.

Christ has transformed the world; He has given it a new, original and inexhaustible source of life. Like the sun, which is far away, Christ supports life with His light and influences our history. The Savior came to transform our lives. At Cana He transformed water into wine. At the end of human history He will transform our bodies into new life (cf. Philippians 3:21; Revelation 22:5). Christ inserts Himself in our history as "the life, the truth, and the way" to orient man towards more sublime destinies, to help man pass from opinions to certitude, to fill man's finite existence with spiritual fullness, to bring about a supernatural transformation of everyone and everything.

The Church has been prepared and authorized by Christ to bring about this qualitative transformation. The Church has always insisted on both the divine and the human elements in man's life. St. Francis of Assisi united the things of this earth to those of heaven; one of the functions of creatures is to be a "cosmic canticle" to their Creator. In this context we find the responsibility of the true Christian. We long for the infinite; we can gather fragments of it in time, in the good impulses of man's heart. The supernatural is part of this world. "All are yours, and you are Christ's and Christ is God's" (1 Corinthians 3:22).

PASTORAL REFLECTIONS

1. *The world needs Christ.* Christianity is above earthly reality, but it is not beyond it. The kingdom of God is not of this world but it is for this world (cf. Pastoral Constitution on the Church in the Modern World, nos. 9, 10). "For the creation waits with eager longing for the revealing of the sons of God" (Romans 8:19). If humanity and every humanistic expression is not united to the absolute values of the spirit, it will not participate in the life of God (cf. Genesis 1:17-18; Hosea 4:3).

2. *The Christian vocation consists in the operative interdependence between the baptismal consecration and social action.* Vatican Council II continually exhorts us to be living elements of the world and life-giving elements to the world (cf. Dogmatic Constitution on the Church, no. 31; Decree on the Apostolate of the Laity, no. 4; Decree on the Church's Missionary Activity, no. 15; and the Pastoral Constitution on the Church in the Modern World). The classical attitude of the Christian has two dimensions: to preserve and to act. He must not be contaminated by evil, and at the same time he must reveal and transform reality with his words, actions and example. His behavior is like that of a man swimming in the sea. He must protect himself from the waves, and at the same time he rests on the waves to reach his goal.

3. *A prayer.* Jesus, my Savior, You have transformed everything into life; help me to sing the wonders of Your love! Help me to be happy, abandoning myself to the light of Your presence. I want to rejoice in Your goodness, which is the source of every good!

I want to be happy, to bring glory to men, to reveal that You can transform all of creation into a gift of salvation!

Jesus, I want to sing Your praise and thank You forever, as You are the source of every grace!

TWENTY-EIGHTH SUNDAY IN ORDINARY TIME

The Catholic Church and Other Religions

Readings: Isaiah 25:6-10
Philippians 4:12-14, 19-20
Matthew 22:1-14

God has so arranged things that all people and every individual can reach Him. He desires "to destroy the veil that covers all peoples" (cf. First Reading). His Providence and goodness are always working to call everyone to the wedding feast (cf. Third Reading). God desires the salvation of all men (cf. 1 Timothy 2:4).

Vatican II, in the Constitution on the Church, teaches that all men are called to belong to the new People of God which is to spread itself throughout the whole world and must exist in all ages so that God's design may be fulfilled. For all men are called to salvation by the grace of God.

Though there are many nations there is but one People of God, citizens of a heavenly rather than an earthly kingdom. All of the faithful, seeded throughout the world with different traditions, are in communion with each other in the Holy Spirit. This characteristic of being universal is a special gift of the Lord to His Church.

Not only is the Church composed of different peoples and traditions, but also of particular churches which retain their own traditions. The Pope presides over the whole assembly of charity and protects legitimate differences, taking care that these differences contribute toward unity. All men are called to be part of this Catholic unity which promotes universal peace in the Spirit of Christ.

We turn our attention first to the Catholic faithful. The Church, a pilgrim on earth, teaches she is necessary for salvation through Christ, the one Mediator and way of salvation. He Himself clearly asserted the necessity of Baptism and of the Church, which men enter through Baptism as through a door. Whoever, knowing that the Church is made by Christ a necessary means, yet refuses to enter or remain in it, cannot be saved.

Fully incorporated in the Church are all those who accept with faith all the means of salvation which the Church offers by way of the sacraments and teaching through her ecclesiastical government of the Pope and bishops. However those who, though incorporated in the Church, fail to respond to Christ's grace and so belong just bodily to the Church, and not with faith and charity, are not saved but will be more severely judged.

Those receiving instruction in the faith or catechumens by their desire to be members are already joined to the Church, and she embraces them with love and solicitude.

The Church is joined in many ways to other Christians who do not profess the Catholic Faith in its entirety or are not in communion with the Pope. These truly Christian people are sealed by Baptism, which unites them to Christ, and receive sacraments in their own churches. Many of them cultivate a devotion to the Virgin Mother of God and celebrate the Eucharist under the guidance of their bishops. These Christians are indeed in some real way joined to us in the Holy Spirit who stirs up a desire that all disciples of Christ may be united as Christ intended as a sign of His abiding presence among us.

We are related to those many peoples who have not yet received the Gospel. First are the Jews, by divine choice a most dear people to God, from which Christ was born according to the flesh. God's plan of salvation also includes Moslems, who acknowledge the Creator; they profess to hold the faith of Abraham and, together with us, they adore the one merciful God.

Those who, through no fault of their own, do not know Christ or His Church but seek God with a sincere heart by striving to do His will according to their conscience, also may attain eternal salvation. Nor does divine Providence deny the help necessary for salvation to those who, without blame on their part, have not yet arrived at an explicit knowledge of God, but strive to lead good lives. So whatever good and truth they may have is in preparation of the Gospel.

But very often there are some left in a state of hopelessness; deceived by the Evil One, they turn their backs on God. Instead of serving God, they idolize their own sinful ways and sadly live and die without God. In her earnest desire to save all the Church takes zealous care to foster the missions—"those who are far off" that they too might "draw near" to the Lord.

As the Father sent the Son in mission, so Christ sends the Apostles saying, "Go, therefore, and make disciples of all the nations. Baptize them in the name of the Father, and of the Son, and of the Holy Spirit. Teach them to carry out everything I have commanded you. And know that I am with you always, until the end of the world" (Matthew 28:19-20).

The Church has received this solemn command of Christ from the Apostles and she must fulfill it to the very ends of the earth. As disciples of Christ we, both laity and clergy, have the obligation of spreading the faith with love and zeal to the best of our abilities (See *Lumen gentium,* nos. 13-17).

PASTORAL REFLECTIONS

1. The most convincing criterion of the veracity of a religion is *the divinity of Christ.* This essential characteristic of Christ qualifies and differentiates Christianity from all other religions. Others, as Buddha, Zoroaster, Mohammed and Confucius, never thought of presenting themselves as a divinity, even if their followers later attempted to deify them. Only Jesus presents Himself as the Son of God, in order to establish on earth His universal kingdom as the Creator and Savior of all men.

2. *A prayer:*
"We believe that the Church is necessary for salvation, because Christ, who is the sole mediator and way of salvation, renders Himself present for us in His body which is the Church. But the divine design of salvation embraces all men; and those who without fault on their part do not know the Gospel of Christ and His Church, but seek God sincerely, and under the influence of grace endeavor to do His will as recognized through the promptings of their conscience, they, in a number known only to God, can obtain salvation" (Paul VI, Credo of the People of God).

TWENTY-NINTH SUNDAY IN ORDINARY TIME

Religion and Politics

Readings: Isaiah 45:1, 4-6
1 Thessalonians 1:1-5
Matthew 22:15-21

Christ's expression "Then give to Caesar what is Caesar's, but give to God what is God's" (cf. Third Reading) leads us to consider the relation between religion and state. In many Western countries this relationship has deteriorated. Church and state are two perfect, complementary societies and there are numerous reasons for the friction.

The first reason is quite evident; both societies have the same subject: man. The point of encounter is not the abstract notion of man's creation but the more qualifying aspects, as instruction, education, marriage, social life and brotherhood. The danger is twofold: there can be a state which tends to enter and regulate the moral aspects of man's life or the Church which wants to control the social life of man.

In order to find the proper solution, we must consider the characteristics of man. When both societies cooperate for the integral education of man, harmony in our society is possible. Both the state and the church are at the service of man, the center of the universe. There are two aspects to man's nature: body and spirit, earthly needs and desires which go beyond temporal existence. Consequently, a state which does not consider the religious behavior of its citizens does them injustice; a state which desires the good of its members should cooperate with religion to satisfy the more profound needs of man.

In practice what does this mean? The state working with the Church should at least try to eliminate moral evil. The Bible has always considered sin in its social dimension. When the religious conscience is done away with, it is simply a question of time before moral and social values will disappear.

In the development of society, it is our theocentric awareness that will give value to that which is Caesar's. Authority which has a democratic origin will be operatively valid only if it is considered in relation to God. Material goods and social justice, the primary interest of the state, can be of value to men only when envisioned and distributed in relation to eternal hope. A true notion of man's dignity can be had only by considering man as the image of God. If the state or the individuals do not recognize this, it is logical that they become aggressive and change the social outlook. Wherever the ideas of divine paternity and our supernatural nobility exist freely, there the things of Caesar can be enjoyed with those of God. The material and the spiritual, even if not interchangeable, can exist side by side for the greater benefit of mankind.

PASTORAL REFLECTIONS

1. *The Church and its members should give a certain tone to society.* Spirituality which does not open to the earthly and social reality is false spirituality. The Christian feels at home in his society knowing that he is making a vital contribution. An old proverb says: "The best way to put up with the noisy celebration next door is to be among the guests." Even though we are citizens of another kingdom, for the time being we must generously participate in our earthly society. St. John Bosco said: "Keep your thoughts on heaven and your feet on earth."

2. *The conscientious citizen benefits both the Church and society.* We must be able to bear fruit wherever we may be. Work, the office, etc., can be seen in relation to their financial value or in the context of the common good.

3. *The advice of the Holy Father* to a group of Christian contractors and businessmen: "You have met to

consider new problems which our evolving society presents. You consider these problems not merely as professional people but also as Christians—that is, as men called to be practical examples of evangelical action. The present moment is a difficult moment; each one of us must make every effort to do his best. We must bring Christian love to the structures of our daily activity; we must assume the entire responsibility of our social positions" (Paul VI, February 12, 1977).

THIRTIETH SUNDAY IN ORDINARY TIME

The Dynamics and Perfection of Altruism

Readings: Exodus 22:20-26
1 Thessalonians 1:5-10
Matthew 22:34-40

Brotherly love, the most difficult aspect of Christianity, is sorely lacking in our world today. The more society extends, the less union there is. Human contact becomes superficial; solitude and inability to love are widespread.

There are various explanations of this phenomenon. Materialism empties and degrades the concept of man. The tendency to consider everything in mass chokes love which is an individual relationship; it also reduces individual responsibility. In an anonymous society the tendency is to pass responsibility on to others. Another obstacle to brotherly love is our insecurity. When we are insecure, we worry mostly about ourselves. Everyone seems to be in a hurry today. This not only renders us nervous, but it does not give us time to consider those who live near us. The rate of change is so frenetic that many people who cannot keep pace are left out. This is particularly true of the older people. If it is difficult to communicate, it is even more difficult to love. Many people do not love, because they are not capable of love. Our cities are full of neurotics and psychotics. At times we have been hurt by the dishonesty of those seeking help but who do not need it; this sad experience dampens our enthusiasm. The principal cause for the lack of love is, it seems, our drifting from God, which has negative consequences on our society.

The way, the intensity and the motivation for brotherly love can be quite varied. We can love others for the sense of satisfaction and social approval which follows. What others think is important. When we are judged to be good and generous, it is easier to be so. If we are despised, we become depressed and less capable of opening ourselves towards others. At times we do good to satisfy a guilt complex; consequently, a great sinner is capable of heroic acts to regain social acceptance. Some say that our ability to do good comes from a natural instinct which urges us to meet the needs of others. The English psychologist Macauley says that the impetus which leads us to love is the example of those who generously and silently love their brothers. This brings us within the boundaries of the sacred.

These motivations are perfected in Christ. His message is "love everyone." The external aspects, such as beauty, riches, intellectual and operative ability, and so on, are partial orientative impulses which lead us to the person, the object of love. The basis of our relations with others is our concept of person. When we respect others as persons, there is no danger that we will use them as means for our neurotic needs; this is true whether they are still in the embryonic phase of life or in advanced age.

PASTORAL REFLECTIONS

1. *Try to see God in others.* Man was deeply hurt when he discovered that the earth was not the center of the universe. He reacted by making every attempt to put man in the center of history through illuminism and the

positive sciences. But man is not just an earthly reality. When we accept our spiritual reality—that is, all men are the dwelling place of God—it becomes easier to love Him and recognize Him as the central value. In a certain sense our fellowmen are "the sacrament of God."

2. *The ability to love is an art.* Human activity has three moments: the possibility to act, the realization of the act and the repetition of the same act. An art is achieved through exercise and repetition.

3. Life would be simpler and happier if there were *more Christian love.* What we need today is an epidemic of generosity. We all have the ability to make the world a little bit better. The goal of our lives is to break the force of egoistic gravitation and enter the orbit of divine love. "The essence of man is to love and be loved" (St. Augustine).

THIRTY-FIRST SUNDAY IN ORDINARY TIME

The Problems of the Priesthood

Readings: Malachi 1:14—2:2, 8-10
1 Thessalonians 2:7-9, 13
Matthew 23:1-12

Problems, difficulties and crises are part of the daily life of the Church and not all the problems come from the outside.

"Risk has taken the place of heroism; success is considered victory. Hedonism has overcome love; materialism has taken the place of love. These changes can also influence the priest" (Paul VI, August 11, 1974).

Another partial explanation of the crisis of the priesthood is the difficulty of the priestly mission. The life of a priest is not an easy life; to be coherent is the hardest part of the life of any Christian.

The fact that some priests have left the priesthood should not cause alarm; the vast majority remain and work for the glory of Christ's kingdom. A Chinese proverb says: "A single tree which falls makes more noise than the entire forest which lives and grows in silence."

We should not be scandalized by the fact that some priests leave the Church, condemning everything the Church has ever done. God, in His divine wisdom, can obtain good from any situation. Our human miseries and shortcomings render us more capable of understanding and accepting the weaknesses of God's people. Christ allowed Peter to deny Him so that he would thoroughly accept and preach the mercy of God. "No one would confess himself to an angel; an angel would not understand us" (St. Francis de Sales). God's grace triumphs because of man's weakness (cf. 2 Corinthians 12:9-10).

The moral weakness of the ministers of the Church is a proof of the divine origin of the Church. Cardinal Consalvi once said to Napoleon: "If our religion could be defeated, we priests would have already eliminated it through our infidelity." Even if the priest is personally unworthy of his mandate, he is always a valid instrument to transmit salvation. The action of any priest is subsidiary; the sole Mediator is always Christ (cf. Hebrews 12:24). Christ uses men to apply the gift of salvation but He does not condition the efficacy of this gift to the personal qualities of the minister. When we receive a gift, we appreciate more the value of the gift rather than the physical and moral qualities of the person who delivered it. We must know how to distinguish between minister and ministry, between investiture and action. In the final analysis we must also remember that the priest is responsible to God for his actions; the priestly character does not render him perfect (cf. First Reading).

The infidelity of some members of the Church might worry us; however, we must never lose faith in God's Providence and patience. This infidelity is both historical and prophetical. The time when the priests of Israel were most unworthy was the very moment when

God promised faithful shepherds (cf. Jeremiah 3:15; 23:1-4; Ezekiel 34:1). Christ does not place hope against suffering, or victory against defeat. Rather He draws faith from our weaknesses and victory from our struggles. Christian faith and Christian hope are not sentiments or emotions; they are the basic attitudes of those who realize that God will never abandon man, and that Christ will always be our strength, our hope and our victory.

PASTORAL REFLECTIONS

1. *The priest must assume his responsibility and love the Church.* "To love the Church does not simply mean to be happy and enthusiastic when everything goes well and the Church enjoys the limelight of public opinion. We must also love the structure of the Church. Man needs human tangible laws; they sustain and stimulate him" (Paul VI, February 10, 1975).

2. *Sanctity is lacking in our world today.* The saints have an instinct for what is perfect. They know how to balance action. They are patient in delusions. They write the history of Christ's kingdom. They can reach the hearts of the most obstinate person, they can impart enthusiasm to youth. In the name of Christ they regenerate their fellowmen (cf. Paul VI, September 18, 1974). The real theologian unites doctrinal orthodoxy to coherent action.

3. *A prayer for priests:*

"Jesus, eternal pastor, hear our prayer for our priests. They are Your preferred followers, the epitome of Your love for souls.

"Jesus, allow only those You desire to become priests. Enlighten those who must choose, counsel, and form. Give us priests who are angels of purity, who are humble and capable of love and sacrifices, apostles of Your glory, saviors and sanctifiers of souls.

"Mary, Mother of the eternal Priest and Queen of the Apostles, procure a perennial Pentecost for the Church through holy and valid priests!" (Pius XI)

THIRTY-SECOND SUNDAY IN ORDINARY TIME
Death and the Christian

Readings: Wisdom 6:12-16
1 Thessalonians 4:13-17
Matthew 25:1-13

To understand the problem of death means to resolve the problem of life.

With His resurrection, Christ confirmed the existence of another type of life. One we know, the other is unknown; one is mortal, the other immortal; one is death, the other is resurrection. Jesus assumed the first and revealed the second. He experienced our death in the first and brought about our resurrection in the second. If He had simply promised resurrection without demonstrating it, it would be very difficult for us to accept His promise. He rose from the dead, and our hope becomes certitude. We should never forget that we have received the gift of eternal life, since we know that Christ obtained our resurrection and justification by His resurrection. "But we would not have you ignorant, brethren, concerning those who are asleep, that you may not grieve as others do who have no hope. For since we believe that Jesus died and rose again, even so, through Jesus God will bring with him those who have fallen asleep...we shall always be with the Lord. Therefore comfort one another with these words" (Second Reading).

The Church is fully oriented towards this supreme destiny. The burial liturgy is full of eternal hope; the day of our death is called the day of birth, the day of life. The pilgrim Church is still far from its homeland but her thoughts and actions are there where Christ is, where eternal life is.

The idea of eternal life is fascinating; it is also a mystery, and, consequently, our human intelligence seeks to know more about it. One question constantly returns: "Do the dead know what we are doing? Are they aware of our existential happenings?" Certainly! The Church has always taught the unity of the Church militant, the

Church suffering and the Church triumphant. Our perfection is achieved by loving our fellowmen always—no one excluded—consequently, also those living in heaven.

Frequently we wonder if we will enjoy the corporeal presence of loved ones in heaven. The resurrection of the body is an article of faith. Jesus said: "The day will come when all those in their graves will hear the voice of God for the resurrection." God created man in view of his final glorification. The beauty God gave our bodies will not be lost. Denial of these truths weakens our faith and diminishes Christian reality.

How will our bodies rise? To help us comprehend the mystery of God's omnipotence, St. Paul uses an analogy from nature: the seed, in its germination process, keeps its essential identity and yet undergoes a radical metamorphosis. "What is sown is perishable, what is raised is imperishable. It is sown in dishonor, it is raised in glory. It is sown in weakness, it is raised in power. It is sown a physical body, it is raised a spiritual body" (1 Corinthians 15:42-44).

In the resurrection, will I have my own body? The body will be different, transfigured, yet it will always be my body. This difference does not mean an absolute separation; between the earthly body and the glorified body there is a vital relation, an element of connection. I know that my personality continues even though every so often every cell in my body is renewed. The renewal of the body in the resurrection will be different, yet it will still be my body.

When we attempt to understand something of the next life a frequent objection is: "No one has ever returned from the dead to tell us how things are." We can answer by saying that silence is the language of infinite love; silence is the attitude of one who is present to serve; silence is the consequence of a spiritual union. Our deceased brothers are united to us as God is. Their silence is an echo of God's silence.

PASTORAL REFLECTIONS

1. *The invitation to Christian hope is both logical and desirable.* Whoever lives this hope is not enticed or disturbed by the things of this world. Even though he must live in a world which is passing he proceeds towards what is stable. As he walks among men he is full of the joy of God. Having lived in this heavenly serenity, when he will be called to end his days he will be calm, knowing that death is the beginning of what he has longed for all his life.

2. The thought of death should set us enthusiastically *on the road of sanctity.* We are travelers, and, consequently, we should have a goal. There are numerous roads and paths, but if they have no destiny they are useless. There can be one of two guides along our earthly journey: vice or virtue. The life of vice offers some pleasure; the life of virtue assures serenity among temporal things and eternal life (cf. 2 Timothy 4:7).

3. The moment of death will be *the most beautiful moment of our existence* if we have lived a life of light and love (cf. Third Reading). The invitation of the Lord to participate in eternal happiness will be absolute joy. "Arise, my love, my fair one, and come away: for lo, the winter is past, the rain is over and gone...let me see your face, let me hear your voice, for your voice is sweet, and your face is comely" (Song of Songs 2:10-14).

THIRTY-THIRD SUNDAY IN ORDINARY TIME

The Spiritual Qualities of Women

Readings: Proverbs 31:10-13, 19-20, 30-31
1 Thessalonians 5:1-6
Matthew 25:14-30

The Scriptures describe the complete man in chapter 31 of the Book of Sirach. In the First Reading of today's liturgy we have a detailed description of the perfect woman.

"A good wife who can find?
  She is far more precious than jewels.
The heart of her husband trusts her,
  and he will have no lack of gain.
She does him good, and not harm,
  all the days of her life.
She seeks wool and flax,
  and works with willing hands....
She opens her hand to the poor,
  and reaches out her hands to the needy....
Charm is deceitful, and beauty is vain,
  but a woman who fears the Lord is to be praised."

Psychology has always taught us that woman has superior spiritual dimensions, that woman has power. Sentiments are integrated in her intellect and will. When she puts herself to something she does so with all her energies. Consequently, her type of greatness will depend on whether she chooses to follow good or evil. Frequently, when a woman chooses evil man will follow her. History is full of examples, beginning with Adam and Eve. John the Baptist was beheaded to satisfy the whims of a woman; Ann Boleyn put Henry VIII on the road to his downfall.

Most women do not choose evil, and, consequently, their influence is positive; the worthy woman inspires, comforts and sustains her partner. Through the centuries woman has been progressing toward regaining her proper position. There is a great contrast between Eve and Mary. The history of the Church lists many great mass conversions; behind most of them is the power of a woman. Constantine was converted through the influence of his mother, St. Helena. Towards the end of the fifth century King Clovis and some three thousand warriors were converted; St. Clotilda played an important role in this event. The Visigoths in Spain were converted, and behind the scenes was Theodosia. It is difficult to say which was more important for Christopher Columbus, the three ships he received from Queen Isabella or the trust and encouragement she gave him.

The influence of a woman is frequently seen in the arts. Dante Alighieri is inspired by Beatrice, Petrarch by Laura, Goethe by Charlotte. Rossini's wife inspired him to write *The Barber of Seville;* Bach was inspired by Magdalen Wilkens; behind Puccini's *La Bohème* is Mimi. Raphael, Rubens, da Vinci and Michelangelo all have great masterpieces reproducing the women who have inspired them. A woman must be herself if she wants to inspire her partner. Women has a marvelous memory, capable of recording both the beautiful and the ugly. It takes very little to set off her deep sentiments.

By her nature a woman is different, and this difference is precious to mankind.

The woman has been created to love, a woman needs to give. A woman is always great if she maintains her nature; there should be equality in values but not in form, equality of rights but not of offices. Woman's liberation should not mean making of her a carbon copy of man; this would be an illusion.

The superior qualities and capacities of a woman are most evident in her exclusive role of mother. "The basic life-giving cell for human society, according to God's plan, is the family. It is in the family that woman can realize and nourish, together with man, her potential ability to receive, give and educate life, thus developing all her abilities" (Paul VI, Nov. 6, 1974).

Because of her deeper appreciation of harmony and beauty, woman is easily sensitive to the presence of God. Her ability to integrate sentiments with intelligence makes it easier for her to enter into communion with God. At the end of Christ's life there are two women present: Mary of Nazareth, born without sin, because she brought the Son of God to the world, and Mary of Magdala, to witness and spread God's mercy.

PASTORAL REFLECTIONS

1. *The woman and the Church.* The Church appreciates and desires the value of a woman. "Woman should become more aware and operative in the knowledge of her dignity. She knows that she cannot be considered simply as an instrument; she demands to be respected as a person both in private and public life" (John XXIII, *Pacem in terris).*

2. *The ecclesial priesthood of the woman.* It is true that the Church has formally excluded women from the ministerial priesthood (Congregation for the Doctrine of Faith, October 15, 1976). Does this mean that the Church considers women as second class members? "Functional difference does not mean difference of dignity in the order of grace.... A tenor choir does not underestimate the value of the soprano voice. It is not a preference of one excluding the other, it is the difference which produces the artistic harmony and beauty.... Even if women do not have the ministerial function they can be active and important in the Church as St. Teresa of Avila, Catherine of Siena, and others. That which is important for the Church is not the person of the minister, but sanctity" (Paul VI, January 30, 1977).

3. *The sacrament of a woman is her maternity.* The apostolic and religious grandeur of a woman is in her maternity, whether physical or spiritual. Men build churches, but women give birth to men. "If I will be saved, it is thanks to the education I received from my mother" (St. Paul of the Cross). The world of tomorrow will not be so much the fruit of the great politicians and statesmen as the fruit of the serious Christian education imparted by the mothers of today.

A mother enlightens and develops every moment of the life of her children. The destiny of a mother is a destiny of love; she gives without limit, she loves in the same way God loves.

CHRIST THE KING

Christ Has Risen for All Times

Readings: Ezekiel 34:11-12, 15-17
1 Corinthians 15:20-26, 28
Matthew 25:31-46

In our religion, the heart, the guarantee, the certitude of every prophecy, of every victory is the resurrection of Christ. Christ's resurrection was the central point of His life. It is the source of hope and grace for the Church. It is the central value of our liturgy. Without the resurrection, our faith would be useless; with the resurrection, our life on earth becomes the history of salvation. It is useful to reflect on the reality of Christ's resurrection, the significance of time and our reply to the Christian commitment.

In this last meditation of the liturgical year let us consider some of the aspects of Christ's resurrection.

1. Jesus foretold His resurrection, thus challenging the confidence of public opinion and history. The resurrection was not a new topic. People spoke of it as a type of reanimation, a return to earthly activity. Christ not only spoke of the resurrection; He gloriously rose from the dead.

2. The resurrection is not the final climax of the Gospels. "This splendid flower has its roots in Jesse; it blossoms in the Incarnation, dies in the passion, and so blooms again in the resurrection that it becomes glory for all men" (St. Bonaventure).

3. Christ's resurrection changed the mentality of His Apostles. For the Hebrews, to be crucified meant to be cursed by God; during the evening of Good Friday the Apostles had given up all hope. Their depression changes into heroic enthusiasm, upon hearing the Good News: "He is risen."

4. An illusion or legend can arise when the fact is desired and expected. Even though Jesus spoke fre-

quently of His resurrection, the people of His times neither understood nor expected it. Mary Magdalen went to the tomb with the intention of anointing the body of a dead man. They were so convinced that He would not return that, when they did see Him, they did not recognize Him immediately.

5. Christ's resurrection is different from that of Lazarus, who regains his previous life subject to death. Christ is glorified. His is a completely new way of being; He is clearly elevated above the reality of His body. Christ had the same body which He incarnated. He still has the signs of the nails precisely to convince the Apostles of this fact. St. Gregory the Great speaks of two marvelous aspects of the resurrection which seem to be contradictory: Christ's body is incorruptible, and yet it can be touched. That which can be touched is by nature corruptible; the incorruptible is a reward of faith. "Through His resurrection, Christ wants to establish a relationship with man that is different from temporal life, namely the relationship of faith" (Paul VI, April 4, 1975).

6. Many of Christ's miracles were in a certain sense obliged by the circumstances. Christ foretold the fact, the time and the way of His resurrection; thus His resurrection authenticates His divinity. The resurrection and the divinity are interdependent concepts; the resurrection leads to the divinity, and the divinity leads to the resurrection. The empty tomb without the appearance of Christ would not have made sense. Likewise the appearances of Christ could have been hallucinations if it were not for the empty tomb. As the Apostles absorbed the fact of the resurrection it became a source of great happiness so that they would shout with joy: "We have seen the Lord. He is truly risen!"

7. Christ, through His resurrection, becomes the Center and Savior of time. Much has been said and written about time. According to the Christian and Biblical way of thinking, time is created by God; it is where the "mystery of salvation" begins, develops, and matures,

that salvation brought about by the power of God through Jesus Christ. The qualitative dynamic ascension of time comes from the resurrection when time was changed from a succession of events to an interior tendency for perfection and the infinite.

PASTORAL REFLECTIONS

1. *Christ's message is a message of life.* The basic message throughout the gospels is life, an abundance of life. Even Nicodemus, who was an older man, was reborn. The Christian who enthusiastically lives his constant rebirth in Christ is a master of time and a creator of life.

2. *The spiritual life grows in the light of God.* Material life began with the separation of light from the darkness; spiritual life is defined in terms of the light of Christ. In the day of judgment the light of Christ's glorified body will be shared with the children of light and distinguish them from the children of darkness. As authentic Christians we are followers and friends of Christ, King of the world and Center of the universe.

3. *A prayer.*

Lord, I want to be among those who risk and give their lives. What good is life if it is not given? If there is no one waiting for me at the end of the road, what good is the road? Help me to seek what is good, to get closer to You!

Lord, help me to accept the life and responsibility You intend to give me. I want to regulate my life on Your word. I want to risk it in Your love. You taught me to believe in love. You taught me to give. You taught me not to trust myself but to trust in You.

Lord, help me to know Your will, to do Your will because it is a will of friendship, of covenant, of sanctity and happiness forever and ever. Amen.

Daughters of St. Paul

IN MASSACHUSETTS
  50 St. Paul's Ave. Jamaica Plain, Boston, MA 02130;
    617-522-8911; 617-522-0875;
  172 Tremont Street, Boston, MA 02111; **617-426-5464;
    617-426-4230**
IN NEW YORK
  78 Fort Place, Staten Island, NY 10301; **212-447-5071**
  59 East 43rd Street, New York, NY 10017; **212-986-7580**
  7 State Street, New York, NY 10004; **212-447-5071**
  625 East 187th Street, Bronx, NY 10458; **212-584-0440**
  525 Main Street, Buffalo, NY 14203; **716-847-6044**
IN NEW JERSEY
  Hudson Mall — Route 440 and Communipaw Ave.,
    Jersey City, NJ 07304; **201-433-7740**
IN CONNECTICUT
  202 Fairfield Ave., Bridgeport, CT 06604; **203-335-9913**
IN OHIO
  2105 Ontario St. (at Prospect Ave.), Cleveland, OH 44115; **216-621-9427**
  25 E. Eighth Street, Cincinnati, OH 45202; **513-721-4838**
IN PENNSYLVANIA
  1719 Chestnut Street, Philadelphia, PA 19103; **215-568-2638**
IN FLORIDA
  2700 Biscayne Blvd., Miami, FL 33137; **305-573-1618**
IN LOUISIANA
  4403 Veterans Memorial Blvd., Metairie, LA 70002; **504-887-7631;
    504-887-0113**
  1800 South Acadian Thruway, P.O. Box 2028, Baton Rouge, LA 70821
    504-343-4057; 504-343-3814
IN MISSOURI
  1001 Pine Street (at North 10th), St. Louis, MO 63101; **314-621-0346;
    314-231-1034**
IN ILLINOIS
  172 North Michigan Ave., Chicago, IL 60601; **312-346-4228**
IN TEXAS
  114 Main Plaza, San Antonio, TX 78205; **512-224-8101**
IN CALIFORNIA
  1570 Fifth Avenue, San Diego, CA 92101; **714-232-1442**
  46 Geary Street, San Francisco, CA 94108; **415-781-5180**
IN HAWAII
  1143 Bishop Street, Honolulu, HI 96813; **808-521-2731**
IN ALASKA
  750 West 5th Avenue, Anchorage AK 99501; **907-272-8183**
IN CANADA
  3022 Dufferin Street, Toronto 395, Ontario, Canada
IN ENGLAND
  128, Notting Hill Gate, London W11 3QG, England
  133 Corporation Street, Birmingham B4 6PH, England
  5A-7 Royal Exchange Square, Glasgow G1 3AH, England
  82 Bold Street, Liverpool L1 4HR, England
IN AUSTRALIA
  58 Abbotsford Rd., Homebush, N.S.W., Sydney 2140, Australia